RIGHT
NOW

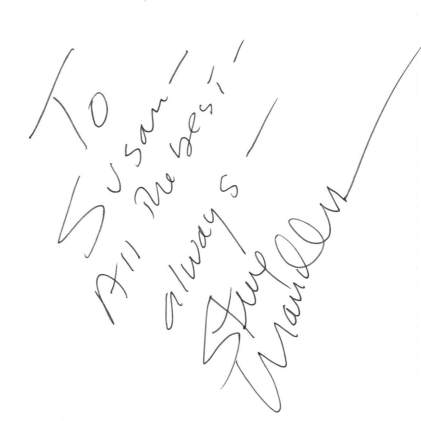

To Susan!
All the best!
always

Steve Marten

Praise for *RIGHT NOW*

RIGHT NOW is my new favorite of all Steve Chandler's books. With his usual humor and easygoing style, Steve shows us that everything we're waiting for is waiting for us in this very moment—beneath the thoughts, labels, identities, and misunderstandings that we carry through life. (He even shows you how to love taking out the garbage—that alone is worth a read.) If you want a brand-new experience of life, I highly recommend you read this book *right now*.

~ **Amy Johnson, Ph.D.,** author of *Being Human* and *The Little Book of Big Change*, and creator of The Little School of Big Change

***

Steve Chandler has knocked it out of the park with his inspiring new book, *RIGHT NOW*. With his use of descriptive and entertaining storytelling, Chandler shows the reader how to wake up to the beauty of life that is available to all of us. If you're tired of waiting for "someday" to have your best life, read this book, not "now," but RIGHT NOW!

~ **Devon Bandison,** author of *Fatherhood Is Leadership: Your Playbook for Success, Self-Leadership and a Richer Life*

***

Steve Chandler powerfully shares his poignant, practical wisdom (with tons of love and levity) to help us see just how simple the mastery of THIS moment can be. True freedom never felt so accessible thanks to this engrossing and entertaining book.

~ **Jason Goldberg,** author of *Prison Break*

RIGHT NOW: Mastering the Beauty of the Present Moment provides penetrating insights into creating and living a thriving life.

~ **Dusan Djukich,** author of *Straight-Line Leadership*

***

Steve Chandler creates yet another masterpiece with *RIGHT NOW*. In this beautifully written, enjoyable and practical book, Steve shares his wisdom and personal stories of how he is a living example of all that he teaches. The message is clear and relevant for all ages: live the life you want now, today, not someday. Be an owner and the cause of what happens in your life. Take action now: pick up the phone and call her, send him that text you meant to send yesterday. Connect with those important people in your life now, *right now*. This book will inspire you and have you taking action even while you're reading it . . . Steve Chandler is a timeless gift for us all!

~ **Sherry Welsh,** author of *Slowing Down—Unexpected Ways to Thrive as a Female Leader*

***

I love Steve Chandler's work! *RIGHT NOW* is a simple yet powerful manual for creating the life you desire and have not yet taken action on. This book provoked thought in a deeply profound and action-oriented way to let go of long-held labels and limiting beliefs to see how I might live and create more in the present moment than ever before. Steve inspires and challenges each of us to let go, slow down and play more with life. Buy this book, read it and use it to see new possibilities for your life!

~ **Kamin Samuel,** coach and author of *Increase Your Abundance Starting Today* and the award-winning *Wealth Transformation Journal*

RIGHT NOW

Mastering the Beauty of the Present Moment

STEVE CHANDLER

MAURICE BASSETT

books for athletes of the mind

RIGHT NOW: Mastering the Beauty of the Present Moment

Maurice Bassett
P.O. Box 839
Anna Maria, FL 34216

Contact the publisher:
MauriceBassett@gmail.com
www.MauriceBassett.com

Contact the author:
www.SteveChandler.com

Editing by Kathryn McCormick
Cover design by Carrie Brito
Interior layout by Chris Nelson

ISBN: 978-1-60025-109-2

Library of Congress Control Number: 2017912666

First Edition

To Kathy

One day you will ask me which is more important?
My life or yours?
I will say mine and you will walk away
not knowing that you are my life.

~ Khalil Gibran

Acknowledgment and Gratitude

To Kathy Eimers Chandler for editing, consulting and making life true and beautiful.

To Fred Knipe for creative consultation, music and friendship all along the way.

To Steve Hardison for years of patient and powerful coaching, and for seeing through my past history and my limiting stories so that we could fly.

To Rich Litvin with gratitude for co-authoring the book that fills the schools, and for making the events in London and California so crazy good.

To my friends and mentors Michael Neill, Dicken Bettinger, and Roxann Burroughs. And to my great teachers Byron Katie, Werner Erhard, George Pransky, Colin Wilson and Nathaniel Branden.

To my publisher Maurice Bassett, and all the coaches and consultants in the ACS, from whom I take daily inspiration.

To the colleagues I love teaching, facilitating and writing with: Jason Goldberg, Rich Litvin, Michael Neill, Ron Wilder, Sam Beckford, Ankush Jain, Carolyn Freyer-Jones and Stephen McGhee.

To my sainted M6 team of extraordinary coaches: Karen Davis, Gary Mahler, Kamin Samuel, Sherry Welsh, Melissa Ford, Tina Quinn, and Devon Bandison.

Table of Contents

RIGHT NOW

She said, "Yes" and I said, "Wow."
And she said "When?"
and I said, "How about right now?"

~ **Brad Paisley**
She Said Yes

Labels That Stick Me to the Past

I was sitting with clients around a table when one young woman told us about her personal life and how she balanced it with work.

During the course of her conversation she talked about nutrition and food and then said softly, "I'm a cake person." She was confessing to a weakness for cake.

But her words hit me like a ton of bricks. What she said. I'd never heard it described that way . . . *I'm a cake person!*

Up until that very moment I didn't know I could *be* a cake person. I thought it was always about the eating of the cake. I assumed I had to discipline myself to eat less cake. I thought it was all about bad choices in the moment. Choices that lead to my plump stomach.

But what if? What if I'm a cake person?

Then when someone points out that I'm violating my paleo diet commitment by eating cake, I can simply let them know that the choice is not mine. Why? I'm a cake person.

I mean, hello! If you're a cake person you eat cake. It's no longer rocket science.

And inside this enlightenment experience I saw exactly

what it is that gets in the way of our unlimited freedom and creativity . . . what produces our inability to thrive inside the present moment.

We can't thrive right now because we are covered with labels. We have labeled and classified ourselves. And the labels have seemed to increase our significance.

But what are they doing really? They've only strengthened our separation from the universe.

We slap labels of permanence and frozen characteristics onto what was formerly unlimited joyful energy. (Watch the family video of yourself running around and laughing at age three.)

We pin ourselves down this way. We chain ourselves up. We end up like those people who enjoy being chained to a big brass bed. We become twisted. We now struggle and strain against life . . . but we are really just struggling and straining against the way we have labeled ourselves.

We say things like, "I'm a cake person. And because of that, and only because of that, when I go to a birthday party or a funeral . . . I eat the cake."

It's a choiceless process. Seamless limitation! Organic captivity!

"I'm a progressive." "I'm a conservative." "I'm a Scorpio." "I'm an atheist." "I'm a foodie." "I'm an introvert." "I'm a 2 on the Enneagram!"

It goes on and on and with each label I get smaller and more paranoid. No wonder all I think about is how I can somehow get into a better future, a better now than this now.

But what's the answer? What's my solution?

Find someone who will steam these labels off my body. And take these chains, as Ray Charles sings, from my heart.

I came to realize that people build themselves personalities as they build houses—to protect themselves from the world. But once they have built a house, they are forced to live in it. They become its prisoners.

~ **Colin Wilson**
Necessary Doubt

Anyone Can Find Someone

I know what you're thinking. You're thinking, What do you mean find someone to steam the labels off of me?

I mean find someone!

It might be someone in a book . . . or someone who does classes on the internet . . . or a spiritual mentor or teacher . . . or a colleague . . . or a grandparent . . . or a friend . . . or someone who has passed away but has left behind audio recordings that will inspire you to be free.

That's what I did. I went from mentor to mentor, hero to hero, inspiration to inspiration. I was finally ready to have them put on full steam. People who saw past the labels to the fearless heart inside of me (and also inside of you too).

And you can even become your own mentor, steaming off labels by entering the silence within. No distractions there. Allowing meditation to occur. Wisdom surfaces. It will be found inside once you get out of the past, get out of the future, and sink into the expanding and infinite present moment.

How present am I willing to be to what's going on? To the person I'm with? To the service I'm providing? To the skill

I'm developing?

These labels drop off the minute I enter the beauty of the present moment. Because to "exist" they require a busy mind continuously spinning stories about the past and spinning worries about the future.

The decision to make the present moment
your friend is the end of ego.

~ **Eckhart Tolle**

You Just Thought You Were Shy

I read an interview with actor Lindsay Pearce, who said, "I was shy and didn't believe in myself, and I only bloomed when I was in theater during rehearsal."

Maybe that *blooming* she did when she was in rehearsal was more of who she really was than the thought, "I'm shy."

The label of "shy" has to be thought up and then maintained. It requires continuous spinning. Like making a circle of light with a flashlight in the dark, it requires that I swing the flashlight round and round so that you, thirty yards away, see a circle of light. Without spinning, there's no circle.

The circle was an illusion. Just as "I'm shy" is an illusion.

To keep the label "I'm shy" going I have to keep spinning memories of the past when I didn't speak up or reach out, and worries about a future of not connecting with people.

I have to actively keep that going in my mind.

"I'm shy" doesn't exist on its own. It has no reality when I stop spinning it. When they do the autopsy they won't find it. It's not there. Even when I give my mind a break and drift into dreamless sleep or reverie it goes away completely. It was never real.

The person who runs across the street into a burning house

and carries a child to safety is so *in the moment* that he forgets his label of "coward" or even his labels of "passive" and "lazy." They disappear in the moment.

The "coward" label has to be *maintained* to appear to exist. It has to be furiously spun. Because it has no existence on its own. As the child who was saved will tell you.

Go into yourself and see how deep the place
is from which your life flows.

~ Rainer Maria Rilke

Swept into the Flow of Your Life

An artist swept into the flow of her painting looks at the clock and is startled to see that an hour has passed . . . an hour that felt like two minutes. Where did the time go?

There is no sense of time when you enter the now.

And when you enter the flow state of artistic creation or craftsmanship the limitation of labels drops away. That's what flow is. The labels themselves don't exist anymore because they are no longer being maintained by a spinning, worried mind. Or a mind always hoping life will get better.

In an interview with *The Daily Telegraph* in April of 1993, Leonard Cohen said, "I've always been free from hope. It's never been one of my great solaces. I feel that more and more we're invited to make ourselves strong and cheerful. I think that it was Ben Johnson who said, 'I have studied all the theologies and all the philosophies, but cheerfulness keeps breaking through.'"

Because cheerfulness is stronger than all the theologies and all the philosophies. It is simpler, too. It's experiential! It flows up strong in the present moment. It doesn't have to figure anything out. It certainly doesn't start looking for a label.

The person who rescued the child from the fire didn't even think it was "he" who was doing it. His energy couldn't help but do it. The fire and the child drew his energy into the present moment.

We see this everywhere and then promptly forget it in the name of label maintenance. Keeping the labels stuck on. Not knowing they are fairy tales. We are thinking they are who and what we are as separately catalogued individuals.

But then every so often we see through it. And the more we open up the more we see through it. It might happen when a spiritual teacher says something unusual and unexpected. Or a song is played that overwhelms us. Maybe it happens when we catch a football with one hand. We start laughing. We quickly feel the pure energy we are made of. The timeless moment is only this sweet because "now" is who and where we really are.

Language gets weird when we flow into the timeless now. Steph Curry has an amazing night of shooting the basketball and his teammates say, "Steph was unconscious tonight." What? But that's sports slang for performing way beyond his norm. Being in the zone. They might also say he was "out of his mind" hitting all those difficult shots.

Why do they use that strange language? Because without consciously thinking it through, they just *see* that something lives beyond linear time.

There's a place beyond linguistic measure. And it's not way out there where Peter Pan used to go. It's hiding right here and it's open for business right now.

My friend, the gifted songwriter Fred Knipe (whose current album *9Ninety9* I use for simultaneous relaxation and inspiration), talked to me recently about this place beyond linear time. He said, "My guitar mentor told me that the goal was not thinking, and ultimately even not concentrating. The music will take off like a kite suddenly lifted into flight. Of course you have to have proficiency just as the kite flyer has to have a path and be able to run. But once you get facility in your hands and have worn out the tedious exercises and scales (the path for running) something outside comes inside the work. If it feels the invitation, the opening."

Your life doesn't transform by consuming insights, but by testing them.

~ Jason Goldberg

What Kind of Future Was I Thinking Of?

It took me a while to realize that the future is right now.

I'll never forget learning this from a mentor who saw that my life was stuck in neutral. "You can go," he would say. "The light has changed," he would point out. And of course he meant the light in my heart.

It had changed.

I would be talking to him about something I'd always wanted to do someday and he would say, "You could do that *right now*." And I then became pretty excited to see that it was true.

Soon I started saying that to myself: *You could do that right now.*

If I had a fleeting yearning to learn Spanish, I would just say, "You could do that right now" and I'd immediately look up the Spanish word for something and I would write it on my whiteboard and say it out loud the next morning.

What I hadn't realized before was that we mentally create barriers to doing that. We don't notice that there's more than one kind of future. One kind has the power to disappoint me by never being fulfilled. But then there's another kind, a better kind of future.

That better future is the one I can start working on right now. I can bite into it this instant, like biting into a stalk of bright yellow corn on the cob. It's the kind of future I can sink my teeth into immediately. The future called right now.

It's not that lonely, stranded future "out there." The one I only think about and heave big sighs over. That one is full of vain hope and sad longing. It's a lost dream, lost at the moment of its first projection.

(Once I thought of writing a whole book about the beauty of the present moment. Then I thought I'd have to wait until I was spiritually enlightened to do it, like Eckhart Tolle, Byron Katie or Rumi. But then I realized that I didn't have to wait for that. I could do it right now.)

When people question the apparent past, they lose their future. The present moment—that's when we're born.

~ **Byron Katie**

Where's the Future Coming From?

Werner Erhard teaches about how to create a life path that works. He talks about creating a future from the future . . . not from the past.

What does that mean? I'll say what it meant for me when I first heard it well enough to use it. It meant that most people (including me) and even most companies plan their future based on the past. They take the past and try to make the future out of it.

Like feverishly beating a dead horse. Whop! Get up! Run!

They would say they were just looking to the past for guidance, but then they put the past on a table in front of them and stare at it and ask themselves, "How can I make this 10 percent or 20 percent better?" So the past is like a lump of clay that is being shaped a little and added to a little. Maybe it's even baked and glazed a little.

But it is still the past.

So when I do it this traditional way, my future is still the past. All I can ever have is a slightly newer, slightly better past. But it's still the past. Do you see this?

That's called creating the future from the past. It's a

remake. It's a sequel. But it's not fresh and new. Life soon becomes a cover band, but not the real thing. Like those casino showrooms that have "tribute bands" playing a whole evening of Pink Floyd or Jimi Hendrix or Journey. There's nothing new and exciting. It is relying on attendees pulling up old emotional memories and trying to nostalgically feel them again.

But what if I chose not to do that? What if I chose to create my future based on a totally invented picture of the future? Something I've never done. Something no one's ever done? Like the hit show *Hamilton*. Instead of just a remake of *Oklahoma.*

This is a future created in the present moment. Right now.

We only have this moment, sparkling like a star in our hand—and melting like a snowflake. Let us use it before it is too late.

~ **Marie Beynon Ray**

A Space Shot to Planet Someday

I was in a seminar many years ago that encouraged me to create a five-year plan for my professional life. At the time I was a company marketing director but I wanted to be a public speaker and seminar leader one day. So I wrote down a plan that might make that happen.

The plan's first year had me taking courses to overcome my fear of speaking in public (a problematic fear if you want to do it for a living). Year two had me doing some short pro bono talks in the community, year three . . . etc., etc. I was proud of the plan.

My friend Steve Hardison (who was later to become my coach and mentor) had attended the same seminar with me and as we were leaving on the last day I told him about my five-year plan. I showed him what I had written down. He looked at it and said, "This is great. But I have a question." I asked him what the question was.

He said, "Why five years?"

I said, "What do you mean?"

He said, "You could do this now."

And I was stunned and startled. Of course I couldn't do it

now. That's the whole point of creating a five-year plan. It's for something that is going to take you five years.

But with his guidance and encouragement, I saw there was another way. I got into immediate action. I compressed my five-year plan into five months and at the end of the sixth month companies and organizations were paying substantial fees to have me come in and speak and train.

Later, after I left that company and Steve became my personal coach, he kept returning to the idea that there's no time like the present. When I would express a vague desire to coach or train some company someday he would reach for the phone immediately and get them on the line. It was terrifying and exciting all at once.

"You've got to pull things from the future," he would always say. "You can't leave them out there. Now is the best time."

It took a long time but I started to see that everything good happens now. Everything I want to do is available right here right now.

My own clients often miss the opportunity known as right now. They hesitate. They worry about whether they might be bothering someone by reaching out to them. So they make a vow to reach out in the future. That future in which they will be better-prepared. The planned-out future!

In other words that non-existent imaginary planet where all great ideas are sent to pile up and rust away. Planet Someday.

Some of us are returning to sanity, because we're tired of the pain. We're in a *hurry*. No time to mess around.

~ **Byron Katie**

Mastering the Beauty of the Present Moment

Today I'm learning to enjoy a satisfying, meditative mindset throughout the day by enjoying every little thing I do. The practice is to take anything that feels like a means to an end and slow down enough to make it an end in itself.

I am beginning to understand what the great songwriter Hoagy Carmichael meant when he said, "Slow motion gets you there faster."

Whether it's taking out the garbage or washing the dishes, I can slow down and have it be an end in itself. Not a means to an end.

If I'm talking to a potential client, I can do the same. If I'm not targeting them as a potential client—a target of opportunity!—(as if my life were a battlefield)—I can enjoy the human connection we have.

I can actually do this with everything. When I make washing the dishes something I need to grind through (a means to an end) I am no longer fully present to what I am doing and I don't allow happiness or satisfaction to be felt until the **end**, a clean sink, is achieved.

So happiness always gets pushed into the future. And the job I do isn't as thorough and complete as it could be. Because it isn't getting any love. It's a means to something else.

I used to live my whole waking life as a means to an end. Everything was something to get through. I raced through everything. If it hadn't been for the restful sleep I got at night I'd have gone insane this way.

Sleep was restorative because once I let go of my thoughts it became an end in itself, and therefore healthy. I didn't notice this at the time. In fact, I even wanted sleep to be a means to an end. I studied ways to hack my sleep so I could make it "powerful." I read up on "power naps." I looked for ways to learn lucid dreaming and impregnate my subconscious with wealth-producing affirmations while I slept! I wanted to work while I was sleeping! But fortunately I was usually too tired to do any of that so I just drifted off at night, allowing my sleep to be just sleep.

I eventually saw how my frenzied, sped-up days were reducing the quality of my life. Everything I was doing all day was a frantic, reckless means to an end. I was doing that because I thought it would mean something good would happen in the future.

This slowing down to appreciate life isn't a new idea. All the great spiritual teachers recommended loving every moment of God's creation. But I always worried about the downside of becoming "spiritual." I had friends who had become spiritual, and yes they seemed happier and more relaxed, but I feared that if I allowed myself to be happy and satisfied with the ordinary day's work, then I'd lose my drive. I didn't want to become a lazy idiot pleased with anything you handed me. I was convinced that my goals would not be reached unless I held my personal happiness hostage to their achievement.

But in doing that I missed something important. I missed the fact that happiness can lead to creativity. Even more so than relentless drive. Happiness is lighthearted and inventive. Happiness invites brilliant, unexpected solutions to pop into my mind. When I'm happy, problems no longer look frightening.

I was wrong to think that happiness would lead to passivity. I didn't understand that it could also invite in a pure and graceful kind of energy.

And I finally caved. I started reawakening a forgotten spiritual path I was on years ago. It was back when I was recovering from addiction and attending 12-Step meetings and seeking conscious contact with a higher power. I wanted those days back again, so I sat with meditation teachers. I read spiritual books. I went to seminars and retreats that my coach recommended.

Soon I started seeing the wisdom in having everything I do be an end in itself. And the more I did that, the more my life got better. Even my profession got better. My prosperity grew. My life changed. All by itself.

If we are willing to stand fully in our own shoes and never give up on ourselves, then we will be able to put ourselves in the shoes of others and never give up on them.

~ **Pema Chödrön**

Life As an End in Itself

Would it really be okay for me to fall in love with taking the garbage out? Or would someone find out about that and put me in assisted living?

There's a phrase that was popular when I was younger and it keeps coming to mind. When a girl in junior high school idolized a film star she would say, "He's the living end."

I love that phrase. The living end. It's the end! No more seeking. It means search no more! Stop right here.

When I used to make "sales calls" in my business, they were a means to an end. I hated them! But I had to do them to get business and make money. So the means were justified by the anticipated end.

But when I learned to slow down, things changed. I myself would slow down, but my success rate would speed up. Soon what used to be sales calls now became an end in themselves. They were the creation of new relationships. Sometimes even friendships!

And people began hiring me faster. The conversations became more relaxed and enjoyable. I was no longer trying to push people into my future. They weren't targets anymore.

I didn't need to execute some kind of manipulative sales process any longer. This moment now was its own process. This moment is always good the way it is. I am here for you right now. It doesn't depend on anything. Let's just talk and see where life takes us. I'll learn about you, tell you about the service I have, and we can see if it's a fit.

And this is where it got strange and wonderful. When someone said "no" to the idea of buying the service I had, I was even happier than if they said "yes." In my mind I went into each "sales" conversation thinking, "A 'yes' would be great and a 'no' is even better." That thought took all the pressure off. It took all the pressure off of both of us. Because my prospective client could actually *feel* my lack of desire to have them do anything other than what they themselves truly wanted to do. Feeling that, they felt free to ask more and more questions and be more and more honest about what they wanted and what they feared. We were creating a relationship.

If this sounds like a sales technique I can only say that it's better and deeper than that. It's a return to the joy of being. Both people realize that they are in the same boat. We are both on the same team. We want the same thing. We want your life to get better. So for me you aren't a means to anything. You are the living end.

I believe I love my guitar more
than the others love theirs.

~ **George Harrison**

Let's Give Everyone a Fresh Chance

Sometimes I like to assign movies for my clients to watch. One of them is *Finding Dory*. The little fish character voiced by Ellen DeGeneres has short-term memory loss in that movie, and much of the humor comes from her forgetting who the other characters are.

She might have a long scene with a character and see the same character two minutes later and have no idea who she's talking to. Then cheerfully she says, "Oh hello! My name is Dory!" How exciting to find a new relationship! And for Dory, they're all showing up as new.

What if I can try being Dory? When I arrive at a gathering and I see someone there who I have had judgmental memories of, this time I approach them as Dory. I am happy and cheerful. I am open and empty and so glad to run into them. There is no story about them that I have to filter their words through.

When I show up empty, I am right here right now in the present moment. Like falling out of thought and like falling in love.

I have to be present to fall in love. Only in the here and now can I fall in love, because falling in love is an experience of pleasant surprise, or, as G.K. Chesterton said about his spiritual awakening, it's like receiving "absurd good news."

And I can fall in love with anything. I recently learned to fall in love with taking the garbage out. I noticed that I dreaded it every week, and when it came time to do it I slogged through it as a means to an end. It never occurred to me that I could make it an end in itself.

So I slowed it down and treated it like a sacred Zen practice. It wasn't long before I couldn't wait until garbage day. I'd even say to Kathy in a voice that sounded like elation, "Tomorrow's a big day."

"Oh really? Why?"

"Tomorrow is garbage day!"

She began to worry about me. She started looking online for what she could find about the first stages of dementia.

It is only stories (elaborate webs of thought) that make it hard for me to give something (like taking the garbage out) or someone (who once said something critical of me) a second chance. Someone criticizes me and I'm caught up into thinking they've done something deliberately hurtful. I try my best to forgive them, but built into my idea of forgiveness is the conviction that I am the person who was right and they are the person who was wrong. When I forgive them it feels like it's big of me to do that. I now sense that from now on I'll never be on the same moral level as they are. My forgiveness elevates my ego.

Isn't that right? Is it not from a superior level that I throw my pennies of forgiveness down to them? A magnificent being ... that's who I am.

Dory would be kinder than that. Dory wouldn't even remember what that other person had done or said. And our love of her character comes not from thinking she's ignorant, but from feeling the kindness behind it all.

Half of life is lost in charming others. The other half is lost in going through anxieties caused by others. Leave this play, you have played enough!

~ **Rumi**

How My Story Builds a Wall

In my experience of recovery from alcohol and drugs I have noticed that some people (who knew me when) never quite trusted or understood that my whole life had changed. I was "that drunk" to them every time they saw me, no matter that decades of sobriety had passed.

I have friends and acquaintances in recovery who are never given a second chance by certain family members because the old stories are stronger than their capacity to forget.

I don't actually regret any of that. It shows me the power of a story. It shows me that stories can prevent a relationship from ever really happening. They can be stories about what men are like. They can be stories about what women really want. These kinds of stories can hypnotize almost everyone alive today.

When I have a story about your political party, or your country, or your profession, who you really are doesn't stand a chance. Whole countries have stories about other countries and will fight to the death because of those stories.

People really enjoy watching *Finding Dory*. They see the love behind giving someone a new start. Maybe the saying

"Forgive and forget" can be shortened, in the interest of time management (and in the interest of love), to simply "Forget." If you did that it would give the people in your world a fresh chance. Your relationship with them would be happening right now and not inside a story from the past.

Feelings like anger or sadness exist only to alert you to the fact that you're believing your own stories.

~ **Byron Katie**

Martin Becomes Addicted to Himself

I usually sell my coaching and consulting service by letting people experience it ahead of time. They then decide whether the experience is worth continuing. It's their decision, not mine. I don't care. I used to care but that got in the way of having a really good conversation.

I used to worry about whether I was qualified to be a coach. I wasn't certified. And was I even qualified? I used to try to prove ahead of time that I was qualified, but that just had me trying to impress people with concepts and claims.

Now I just jump right into the present moment and see if I can help.

Like with Martin.

Martin's little one-man law practice was a mess. (Martin is not his real name. None of these names are real. Only the stories are real. Like the old TV show used to say, "There are eight million stories in the naked city . . . this is one of them.")

Martin's bookkeeping had gotten out of hand. He was cash poor but he also had invoices he hadn't sent out for weeks at a time. Invoices for his up-front retainer fee went unpaid even though he had begun working with the clients.

He hired me to coach him. And once again it caused me to wonder, *Why am I qualified to coach people?* I'll never know. But maybe I will never have to know. "Unqualified" is just a passing thought and label. So good to see that all thoughts are just passing through. Why grab them and paste them on my forehead like stickers?

My experience had showed me that people's problems occurred because of those labels. The labels become what they think of themselves. Who they think they actually are. That's why my work is often helping people see that those labels can be removed. Not after years of counseling or decades meditating in a Himalayan cave.

But right now.

Like Martin and his pile of invoices that have not gone out. You'd think he has a bookkeeping problem, but Martin thinks not. He thinks he has a Martin problem.

"I'm not a detail person," he tells me.

He thinks I'll accept that label without question. After all, who knows Martin better than Martin?

I don't know Martin that well yet, but I know labels. They can be removed.

So I ask him to tell me what he means.

"I'm not a detail person," he says. "That's why my bookkeeping is in such disarray. I have never been a detail person."

"What kind of person are you?"

"Oh I don't know. More of a big picture person. Like a visionary, I think. My mother said I was a dreamer."

He then told me his astrological sign to add scientific-sounding punctuation to the information. I think he said he was a Pisces. Maybe he thought that should be enough of an explanation right there.

He didn't see that the story was made up . . . made up on the spot every time he told it. It was a story that left a tornado of unpaid invoices in its wake, scattered around his world like debris. It was a story that left him cash poor and thinking he needed a coach. He was, in effect, pointing to his forehead and saying, "Hey, read the label!"

In Martin's mind there was finality and permanence in his view of himself. He shrugged his shoulders and said, "We're all stuck with who we are, no?"

"No," I said.

Martin wasn't really stuck. It just felt that way to him. He had merely misinterpreted something. A tiny flake of confetti in the wind known as thought had been seized upon. It was then inflated and added to until it became a full-blown belief: "I am not a detail person." Its origin was an arbitrary, passing thought. Just passing through.

Maybe he'd heard someone say that phrase "detail person" and it became a memory. It swirled back in whenever he saw chaos and soon it began to take on shape and significance. He infused it with meaning. Today, as he talks to me, he believes it. He believes it is a solid feature of permanent Martin!

I wanted to be direct with him because beating around the bush wasn't going to help. Beating around the bush would complicate our work together.

I said, "It's nonsense."

"What's nonsense?"

"You not being a detail person."

"Oh really? What kind of a person do you see me as?"

I told him I saw him as a person made of possibility. He was made of anything and everything he could imagine.

"But what about the invoices?" he said.

"All you need is a system. That's all that's missing. It has nothing to do with who you are. It would be a system anyone could use. Anyone. A Pisces, a Sagitarius, anyone."

"A system," he said. He was skeptical.

"A system for invoicing. One that is simple and functional."

He still couldn't believe that this problem really had nothing to do with his identity as a person. He was like most of us. We believe all our problems originate from who we are as personalities. It's all about our personal identity and characteristics. And that's why those problems are so hard to solve. We see ourselves as solid entities that produce problems. If the problems get too big or too numerous, sometimes we don't even want to live anymore. We don't realize that at any given moment (such as right now) we can become pure possibility.

I suggested a system to Martin.

I said he didn't have to stick with the system I recommended. He could always replace it with another system if he wanted to.

"But try it out," I said. "Are you willing to give it a try?"

"Of course."

"Okay here it is: When someone buys your services, invoice them immediately. Right then. The moment they say they are hiring you. Your client might say, 'Okay I'm in, send me an invoice for your retainer' and you will say, 'I'll do that *right now,*' and you do it. You always do it that way, with no exceptions. All invoices are to be sent immediately. No lag time. Don't even get up to use the bathroom before the invoice goes out. Buy a catheter if you need to."

He agreed to do that for the next month. It was amazing

how well it worked for him. A lot of months have passed since I had that session with Martin and he tells me he still does the system.

There are so many things we think are deeply personal that aren't. There are so many things we could do right now if we realized that we ourselves are not the problem. Our labels are the only problem.

The worst thing you can think about when you're working is yourself.

~ **Agnes Martin**

A System Is Just a Dance

A system is a series of simple dance steps. It doesn't have to be the right system, or the system prescribed by someone. It just has to work for you. The simpler it is, the better.

Because anyone can dance. Watch those little children when you put the music on! Without lessons!

You, too, can just put on some music inside yourself. Or meditate for a while until you hear the music . . . the songs of distant universes beckoning you out of your personal thoughts.

Katrina was a powerful public speaker and consultant. Her life was rolling along nicely except for one little secret she almost wasn't going to tell me.

And I tell you her secret because of the point I think it makes about the awakening available to us now. It has to do with mastering the beauty and utility of the present moment.

In other words, there are always things we can do right now.

Katrina kept hitting the snooze button in the morning. She never got up and out of bed at the time she wanted to and had planned to. So she started each day feeling like she was running behind.

I asked her why she thought this was happening. Because I knew her to be an otherwise productive and effective person.

Something inside her, she said. Some hidden memory from childhood when she learned of someone's death one morning while in bed, and never wanting to get out of bed from that day forward. It wasn't conscious, over the years. She just kept noticing that getting out of bed was a complete struggle. Every day!

I decided to try something abrupt. I told her I had a cure for this if she was open to experimenting. As always she was eager to try.

I said, "You don't get out of bed for only one reason. And it has nothing to do with your memory, although I understand how painful that event was, and the pain that memory calls back."

"Okay," she said, "What's the real reason I don't get out of bed?"

"You don't get out of bed because you don't get out of bed."

Katrina was silent. Then she said, "That's it? I don't get out of bed because I don't get out of bed?"

"That simple."

She said, "You are going to have to say more about that because I am not following you."

I told her I could talk forever about it, and we could debate intellectual concepts about psychology, but this was something she would have to learn on the experiential level. Or she would never see it.

So I asked her if she was willing to do a two-week experiment. She said she was. She said this may be the biggest problem in her life, and she was internally embarrassed about it. Always. Every day she was running behind.

I told her that her assignment was to get out of bed the moment the alarm sounded. Just as she would if she worked at a fire station and the alarm came in. Exactly like that. If she had thoughts about sleeping just a little bit more, she was to notice those thoughts but get up anyway. Could she do that each morning for two weeks?

She said she would do that.

I said, "You're not getting up because you're not getting up. That's all that's happening."

When we talked two weeks later she was happy and excited. She got up every morning right when she planned. The alarm sounded and she was up. Some mornings the thoughts came in, but before she could think them over she was already up, on her way to the coffee maker and the day ahead. She could hardly believe it. How could it have been that simple?

We all have things about ourselves that we believe would take forever to untangle and heal. We imagine a future of working on ourselves. Then we imagine the past and how it seems to cause everything. We don't even consider what could happen if we just jumped into the beauty of the present moment.

We binge-watch our painful memories, and then we feel embarrassed and helpless. So we switch to thoughts of the future and soon become anxious and fearful. Whatever we picture in the future seems to contain a lot of challenge and hard work.

But this is all just thinking. Why not just get up? The present moment always has opportunities like that on offer. And it never requires a lot of thinking. When you live in the present moment there's never a lot you have to try to figure out.

I don't have a past. I have a continuous present. The past is part of the present, just as the future is. We exist in time.

~ **George Balanchine**

Beware of the Judgment Cascade

People often tell me they have an inner critic. They would love to live in the now, but there is this voice that judges them. This "inner critic" always labels them in a negative way.

"You're a mess." "You're a weakling." "You're an incompetent." "You're a loser." "You're not a good provider." "You're not a good parent."

Even though these are just fluttering thoughts passing through, they can seem like the voice of an actual inner person. Sometimes this voice can be like a frontier-era hanging judge.

Adam Phillips wrote about this inner critic in striking terms when he said, "Were we to meet this figure socially, as it were, this accusatory character, this internal critic, we would think there was something wrong with him. He would just be boring and cruel. We might think that something terrible had happened to him. That he was living in the aftermath, in the fallout of some catastrophe. And we would be right."

I get where he was going with this personification. He wanted to dramatize how absurdly unfair and inaccurate this "personage" was. He wanted us to see that we were better than that. And that the inner critic need not be taken to heart.

But of course the inner critic is just a thought. There's no critic in there, really. You have just learned to think there is.

But it's only (and always) just one thought after another. That's all it is. And the moment I give the first critical thought significance another thought arrives, a judgment about that judgment. So now "You're not doing enough" is joined by "You were never good enough" and then "Your father and mother never gave you the tools to live a good life with" and then "But therapy was supposed to heal that" and then "You must not have done therapy right . . . you resisted . . . you were a coward . . . you don't know how to be vulnerable . . ."

And now we have a cascade. A judgment cascade.

It started with a single judgment, which was only a thought passing through. But it was seized as truth and then it gathered into a cascade, thought upon thought upon thought. No wonder it feels like a full-blown inner critic!

I have a friend who criticizes herself a lot. When I point out that a certain criticism might not have any merit, she can see that to be true, but rather than relaxing into that happy insight she immediately judges herself for having criticized herself to begin with.

"Why do I do that?" she says. "What's wrong with me that I'm so critical of myself?"

If I say, "Look, there you go again!" she feels worse, bringing more and more of the cascade of thinking down upon her innately free and easy spirit.

It's good to beware of the judgment cascade. To know what it is and how it can happen. Now you can see it for what it is when it happens. Just thoughts. You don't have to make it into a creepy character that lives inside you. My inner critic!

Remember that it all started with a single thought. A thought like "I'm not a detail person" or a thought like "I can't get up in the morning." There is no need to turn those passing thoughts into something they aren't. Settle down and they're gone.

When our understanding of the play of thought allows us to stand open and receptive in the face of any thought whether of love or grief, and it flows through us naturally, then a deeper unconditional love arises that embraces all of life as it is and it flows out of us to touch those around us.

~ Dicken Bettinger

Like Gentle Rain from Heaven

When Shakespeare first saw the true role of thought in our lives he wrote, "There is nothing good nor bad but thinking makes it so."

When I see that for myself I don't have to obsess and brood over my own self-criticism. I don't have to give weight to a self-critical thought (unless it reveals an opportunity for a new course of action). And I certainly don't have to invent a ghostly personage inside of me called "my inner critic" that I now believe dwells forever in some dark place in my psyche.

With the knowledge that a thought is just a thought, I can show myself mercy. True mercy, and not some forced affirmation that tries to convince me that I "love myself."

As Portia says in Shakespeare's *The Merchant of Venice*, "The quality of *mercy* is not strained. It droppeth as the gentle rain from heaven . . ."

Mercy is not strained. Which is why so many of my attempts at positive self-reprogramming didn't last. It was very strained. It didn't just drop in.

In the grade school my children attended in Arizona the gymnasium had a slogan painted in huge letters on the wall,

"IF YOU HAD FUN YOU WON."

My mindset at the time was a little constricted. I thought sports were only about winning. So I didn't like that slogan. I thought it might encourage kids not to play to win. I never said anything about it. I didn't go to the principal or anything. I let it go. But I cringed every time I saw it.

Today I love the gentle wisdom in that slogan. It's not something I have to affirm to myself constantly. I just see it now that the fun of playing is the whole point, especially when we're talking about playing the game of life.

When you have exhausted all possibilities,
remember this–you haven't.

~ **Thomas Edison**

You Can Do It Right Now

To me, it was a true revelation: There are things you can do right now.

I know that doesn't sound like big news. But I still like breaking it to people. Because it's not something they always notice.

Tamara said to me, "I want to have a better relationship with my mother. She lives back east. I don't talk to her very often."

"Why don't you call her?"

"I keep meaning to."

"How about right now?"

"Right now? I'm in a coaching session with *you* right now."

"Yes, but we are working on improving your relationship with your mother. So call her. I'll get off the line. We can pick up after your talk with her."

And so the new relationship between Tamara and her mother began. In that present moment. Not in our always well-meaning future. A much better use of time than me talking to her *about* calling her mother.

There are so many things in life like Tamara's relationship with her mother. Things we can do right now. Honoring the opportunity inside the present moment. Mastering its beauty.

For example, I love how Isaac Asimov wrote his books. He wrote over 500 books! Can you imagine? What about writer's block? Where did that thought go? Asimov wrote many bestsellers, like the *Foundation* series. I know that his output was absurd, and few writers really aspire to that level of productivity. But I love reading in his autobiographies (he actually wrote three of those) about his writing habits.

His favorite thing to do was to be writing *right now*.

It was his secret system of productivity.

If he was sitting in a doctor's waiting room and there were ten minutes more before his appointment, he delighted in that, and pulled out his notebook and wrote a short chapter for his current book. He wrote anywhere and everywhere throughout the day. He didn't have a sacred sanctuary of time set aside for his writing.

Or, actually he did, and it was called the present moment. That was his sacred space.

What is it *you* always wanted to create? What if you set this book down and started it right now? Would that upset your apple cart?

This opportunity can be applied to the relationships in your life, too. Who in your life have you neglected? If I asked you to name someone in your family, or an old friend who you have lost touch with—someone who, when you think of them, a tiny shiver of guilt passes through you—who would that be? It's not a good feeling, I know. What if you just contacted them? What if it was no longer a big deal that had to be thought about forever?

We often turn things into a big deal by blowing them up

and floating them into the scary future. We fill these tasks with helium. Their importance and significance expands. Now they seem too big to hold on to any longer, so off they go into the distant future.

"This is too big. I can't do this right now."

There's a poster up in the gym I go to that shows a boxer strapping on a glove, and the poster says WHO'S STOPPING YOU? I love that poster. I love that question!

One must still have chaos in oneself
to be able to give birth to a dancing star.

~ Friedrich Nietzsche

A Blind Pig Goes to Mexico!

When I was nineteen years old I took a bus from Detroit to Mexico City.

I had been kicked out of college (or at least suspended) because of bad grades which themselves were a result of drinking instead of studying. My father thought it would be a good idea for me to go to Mexico and learn Spanish and not just slack around during my suspension, and I agreed.

In those days I was pretty clueless about how the human mind worked. But even a blind pig finds an acorn now and then.

I was looking forward to going to Mexico and learning Spanish, so I was in a good state of mind. And so somehow some wisdom from above (above my usual low level of consciousness) spoke to me and said "Don't wait. Even though you will be enrolling in a *Curso Intensivo* a week or so after you arrive in Mexico City, you can start learning Spanish *right now*!"

Who was stopping me?

So I found a workbook for learning Spanish in a bookstore and packed a backpack and boarded the bus. It was a long ride down there from Detroit to Mexico City, but I kept myself busy working in my workbook. By the time I got off the bus I was completely surprised at how much Spanish I could understand. When the actual course began I had a head start and was able to enjoy the learning so much more than if I had gone in ice cold with no feel for the language. The other people in the class thought I must be super bright because I was catching on so fast. But I'd simply not waited (as they had) to be introduced to the language.

Unfortunately, grasping the power of now didn't stay with me. It didn't become a functioning part of my life. It would be a long while before it became a gift that I was aware of on a day-to-day basis.

Yes there were always glimpses along the way, but I didn't pick up on them.

This was one glimpse: Once in Toronto while visiting my lifelong friend Terry Hill (who would later co-author five books with me) I sat with him at his dining room table while he worked on an ad campaign for a company that made watches. The rough artist's sketch he was working with showed someone opening a gift-wrapped wristwatch. He'd come up with the lines, "There's no time like the present . . . and *there's no present like the time.*"

How many times would the universe have to send me that message before I got it?

If I don't manage to fly, someone else will.
The spirit wants only that there be flying.

~ Rainer Maria Rilke

After Decades of Laziness
and Confusion

There's no greater gift than the present moment. But it sure took me a long time to understand that. I almost ran out of life before I saw that.

It wasn't until my late forties that I had the good fortune to hire my life coach and business coach Steve Hardison. My career as a public speaker and coach was going nowhere until he came along and gave me the guidance I needed to make it work. Although to simply call it guidance would be understatement.

One of Hardison's recurring teachings in his work with me was a healthy disrespect for the future. Any time I had something I wanted to do in the future, he would show me how to reel it back into the present moment, like some big fish that had taken the line and run with it.

I remember when this was completely new to me.

My habit was to be continuously letting my plans and intentions swim off toward Someday Isle (as in "Someday I'll start a coaching school" or "Someday I'll write a book" or "Someday I'll . . .") but he would bring me back to the place where all creation occurs: right now. Our sessions uncovered the beauty of the present moment.

Even in little things, he'd always bring me back to the now. If I mentioned the name of someone I wanted to work with, or a company I wanted to bring my training to he'd immediately reach for the phone. Right then! In that very moment! Wait! What the . . . ?

"What are you doing?" I would say.

"We are calling them right now!"

"But I can't do that, I'm not prepared! I don't know what to say to them. I've got some fears to work through. I need to process some feelings . . ."

"Don't worry about that," he would say. "If you can't do it, I'll be you. I'll call and say I'm you."

And he would call and talk to them. He wanted me to see that we didn't have to wait and it wouldn't matter to them which "Steve" they had talked to on the phone as long as I got the appointment and I could then show them my stuff.

I'd say, "But what if they remember your voice? My voice is lower than yours. When they meet me they might notice!"

He would laugh and say, "They'll just think you've manned up! They'll admire you even more!"

It wasn't long before I was making those calls myself. He showed me the way. Because I finally understood that it was never about the exact words he said to them. It was always the fact that he'd reached out with such enthusiasm that made things happen.

After a while I'd lost the habit of always feeling unprepared. Unprepared! In the past, that's always what stopped me. I was never ready. I always thought I needed more time to prepare!

And it was exactly that thought that produced the fear.

The thought: "I'm unprepared!"

The feeling: fear.

It's always the thinking we have, isn't it? That's what gets the fireball of death rolling inside us. We think it's the feeling that does that but it's the thought.

I'd always had that reversed. And because I had it reversed I was afraid to venture out into the world and do things. Better to just stay home and think about the circumstance that caused this feeling.

Subconsciously I was afraid that if I ventured out into the world I would only encounter more circumstances. I might even run into some intimidating people! It's probably safer to be home alone.

When I did get the courage, or the survival instinct, to venture out it was always on a mission of pleasing, flattering and disarming people so that they would like me and maybe even pay me. It makes sense, looking back. If I thought the source of all my bad feelings was other people and circumstance, no wonder I would try to disarm them. Flatter them. Keep them at arm's length. Be afraid of them.

But when I saw that a bad feeling can *only* come from a thought inside me, then other people became less intimidating. In fact, I began to see that they were just like me. They were living in the feeling of *their* thoughts. I understood them now. In a weird way I felt I understood them even before I met them. So it became easier to invite them into the present moment and talk.

We don't need to create love, or well-being, or happiness, because love, well-being, and happiness are part of our essential nature. We don't need to learn to open our heart or connect with others, because that's just what happens when we don't stop it from happening.

~ **Michael Neill**

I Had Too Much to Think

Recently my daughter called me because she had been watching a video interview with the psychologist Rohini Ross in which Rohini answered a question about something in her past that was upsetting to her. Rohini said she was upset because she "had a lot of thinking" about the situation.

My daughter already knew that in theory situations themselves don't cause feelings. Only thinking can do that. But even though she understood the theory, and could see how that was technically probably true, she never really *got it* till that very moment when Rohini Ross said those words: "I had a lot of thinking about that."

My daughter said, "I always thought I just had fears. That the fears were first. And they caused the thinking. I had it backwards."

We're fools whether we dance or not,
so we might as well dance.

~ Japanese Proverb

Why Do I Feel Unprepared?

There's a bluegrass folk song I've always loved called "Banks of the Ohio." In the song the singer holds a knife against his lover's chest, and she cries, "Oh, Willie, don't you murder me, I'm unprepared for eternity."

Unprepared for eternity! That thought creates a fear of death. But it's so good when I see that that fear doesn't come from death itself. (As we all think it does.)

So once not long ago I sat in the office of Steve Hardison and announced to him my idea for a book I wanted to write. It was a good idea but not a great one, and he could tell I wasn't too excited about writing it, but I liked it well enough to do it.

He then asked me what was the book I was afraid to write. The one that would be like none of the other books. What was the book I was secretly longing to write someday but right now felt not quite ready to do?

I immediately knew what it was. It would be a book about my history with addiction to alcohol. A book about addiction, suicide and death. I even knew that the title would be *Death Wish* if I ever wrote it.

He lit up. He said, "Write *that* book!"

What, right now?

I started thinking, "I mean, I'd have to give that a lot of thought. I don't know if I'm ready to write about such a potentially painful and even embarrassing subject. I should probably pray about this. At least meditate. You don't want to rush into something so personal."

He just kept staring at me.

The book was started that night.

I've never had a book get the response that book has received . . . people reaching out to me from all over the world . . . family members of addicts and addicts themselves who allowed that book to touch them and give them new hope. No other book has done that to that degree.

What if I had waited? Those people would not have been touched. And I'd still be waiting. I'd be waiting until the time was perfect. Meaning never. In my inner world, "perfect" is another word for never.

I'm glad I wrote that book when I did because if I had waited too long I might have passed away while writing it, and everyone would say, "How ironic and sad that the book he was writing when he died was called *Death Wish*. He probably brought it on himself."

If I waited for perfection I would
never write a word.

~ **Margaret Atwood**

Wandering into Life Unprepared

In one of my sessions with my coach I let it drop that someday I'd like to form a school for coaches.

I'd found that when I talked to coaches about their practices they said they had a hard time selling their services, even though they were really good coaches. The more I talked to them the more I realized that there was a fundamental confusion about what their clients were actually buying. Once that confusion got lifted, it was clear sailing to prosperity.

"I bet I could teach a whole school of coaches this thing called enrollment," I said to my coach. "Enrollment as a focus on serving instead of selling. Because when I've coached individual coaches they each learned a version of the same breakthrough. So I bet I could teach a whole roomful at once."

You can guess what he said. He said I could do that right now. And by right now, he never meant later this year, or this month, or even sometime this week. He meant right now.

So in that same hour we created the basic program, the dates it would be held, what it would cost, and who I'd like to start inviting. That afternoon I started inviting coaches to the school, and here we are over ten years later and the school is going strong.

"How long did it take you to create and develop this thing?" many coaches have asked me, and I always automatically say, "Years." But in truth it took minutes. When I look back honestly.

If I'd been working with any other coach, this is the thought that would have been given the royal treatment of deep respect: "This school is going to take a lot of careful planning. I need to be well prepared before I launch it."

Not long ago I listened to a webinar wherein one of my favorite authors and teachers, Dr. George Pransky, talked about his early days of going into organizations to teach them his psychological principles that led to greater performance, productivity and morale. There were many times when he was at a loss for what to say to his audience. Learning about the nature of thought and about the importance of their employees' state of mind seemed off-subject. The group wasn't getting how his teaching related to performance and their team's productivity. Telling the story, Pransky laughed and said, "We were in over our heads!" But that didn't stop him. He hung in there until they got it. They needed those breakthroughs right now. They didn't have the luxury of waiting until he was fully prepared to connect with them.

He also didn't see anything wrong with being in over his head. The opportunity to make a difference was right now, not in some overly-prepared, guaranteed-outcome future. (That future we're all looking for.)

My friend Fred Knipe, who is a genius songwriter and a wildly entertaining comedian, created a comic persona named Dr. Ludiker. The humor of Ludiker is in how unqualified (and unprepared) he is to give advice. Yet he gives it freely and buoyantly even though the advice is all bizarre and hilariously incorrect. Audiences love this character. They laugh long into the night when Fred performs. His act is in great demand.

I think they are almost shocked at his character's childish arrogance in delivering wisdom based on nothing. They love someone being that unprepared and still pressing on with wild, unjustified confidence. Always in over his head!

Dr. Ludiker is like the Charles Dickens character Pickwick, who, in the words of G.K. Chesterton, "goes through life with that god-like gullibility which is the key to all adventures. The greenhorn is the ultimate victor in everything; it is he that gets the most out of life . . . His soul will never starve for exploits or excitements who is wise enough to be made a fool of."

That's it exactly. He is wise enough to be made a fool of. That's the wisdom of not needing to look prepared. Just thriving on the moment at hand.

I have met on the street a very poor man who was in love. His hat was old, his coat was out at the elbows, the water passed through his shoes, and the stars through his soul.

~ **Victor Hugo**

Let Me Take You Down
and Lift You Up

Falling in love is the experience of returning to the eternal now.

When I'm in love, where else would I rather be but right here right now? It's a form of being "out of my mind." Falling out of my mind into a moment of truth I was not expecting.

Love, truth and beauty seem to be at the heart of all this. Because many other beautiful, amazing things inspire the same drop into the present moment. A sunset in Tucson. A street full of autumn leaves in Michigan. A certain painting, a sad and beautiful song. Holding my new grandson in my arms. They all take me down, or lift me up into the beauty of the present moment.

What if we could live there?

What if we already live there?

The best way to find yourself is to lose yourself in the service of others.

~ **Mahatma Gandhi**

Branding Myself Versus Serving Others

The life coaches and business coaches I knew and invited into the school were making the mistake of trying to sell themselves to clients. They were, like in high school, overly focused on themselves and how they were coming across. They worried excessively about their own images and "credibility." They were always painfully aware, in conversations with prospects, of how they were looking to the other person. The spotlight was turned on them.

They were trying to make an impression.

It wasn't long before they even became tangled up in trying to make decisions about their "personal branding." When their prospects weren't buying the coaching they went deeper into examining themselves, correcting and redefining themselves. Soon their most common worry, in moments of candor, was whether they were "frauds." Some of them told me they had "worthiness issues."

They were all looking in the wrong direction.

It was as if they were astronomers who woke up each day to use a telescope, but always had it pointed the wrong way.

No wonder they couldn't see the stars.

Here is what the coaches were not seeing: What a prospect really buys is an experience, not a person. They buy how they feel after the conversation with the coach. They buy their own internal insights. They buy real and true possibility.

But very few coaches understood this, so they'd continuously try to make an impression. They would be *impressive* in their conversations with prospects. After these first conversations prospects would often email one of these coaches and say how impressive the coach was. No wonder they saw that. The coach was putting everything into being impressive. Prospects would even say, "I can see why people want to work with you."

But these same prospects decided to take a pass on being coached. Because they realized at some level that it's a lot of money to pay to just be impressed by someone.

My school was formed to help coaches and consultants turn the telescope around. So that it's not pointed at yourself. You learn to look, instead, into the person you are talking to.

You can go on a voyage of discovery. Eventually you'll connect with the person you are talking to, not your own image. Because the person across from you is no longer a means to an end.

You are no longer trying to manipulate that person into your financial future. Together you are sharing the here and now.

When I used to work in advertising we had a term called "gross impressions." If you rent a billboard on the highway and put your message up there you want to know how many cars drive past it each day. Those were called "gross impressions." As I worked with coaches that phrase kept coming back to me. Because in the client enrollment process, impressions are gross. Trying to be impressive is gross. It's a turn-off. It's the opposite of what you want it to be.

It reminds me of the joke about the guy in the bar trying to impress the woman on the stool next to him. He drops a quarter to the floor, and twists down to pick it up and says, "Excuse me, sorry, I just dropped my Congressional Medal of Honor."

Coaches would say, "So if I'm not supposed to make an impression, how do I show up? What do I do?"

You show up empty. You enter the now. You have no agenda. You're a compassionate listener. You talk when you think it would help.

That system worries some coaches at the beginning. But soon they start getting clients at a faster rate than ever. That's been the experience of the school. Prospective clients come away from the conversations excited about what they saw . . . in themselves. Not in the coach. They are inspired by new insights and possibilities. And they're not intimidated by the coach at all. In fact, that's what they like. They often say they want to work with the coach because the coach understands them. They feel connected with someone they can relate to. They didn't really want to work with a superior being.

A human will do just fine.

So coaches learn to jump right in and serve the person. Like a paramedic would if someone were hurting. If someone were lying on the floor twisting in pain, the paramedic wouldn't kneel down and say, "Before I do anything for you let me tell you my history . . . where I was trained, where I went to school, how many lives I've saved, how I view the healing arts . . . what my core values are."

People make fun of the coaching profession (not as much now as they used to, but still they do . . .) because it looks so unqualified. A psychologist has to have extensive schooling and degrees and certifications, and there are strict regulations, whereas a coach just has to say she's a coach and it's *game on*. Your Uber driver can be a coach just by saying so during the ride. You can send him your money and start working with him that very day. How reputable a profession is that?

But here's what the outside world unfamiliar with coaching doesn't understand. Coaches have to actually help people. Coaches have to make a real difference in people's lives or else they go out of business. They even have to make a real, positive difference in those initial conversations or they don't even get hired. A coach has to be useful and helpful to people in order to remain a professional coach.

A psychologist or a psychiatrist does not. They can have patients referred to them forever whether they make a real difference or not. Much of this is based solely on society's longstanding traditional respect for their credentials.

A coach in our school will say, "I have a conversation lined up tomorrow with a person I'd really like to have as a client. What should I do?"

I can only answer them by sharing what works. Show up empty. And don't waste time on preliminaries and posturing and making an impression. Don't try to wait for them to pay you in order for them to experience what coaching is really like. You want to see if you can help them right now.

If your daily life seems poor, do not blame it; blame yourself that you are not poet enough to call forth its riches; for the creator, there is no poverty.

~ **Rainer Maria Rilke**

I Cannot Create Abundance

"I cannot create abundance. It already exists everywhere.
The only thing I can create is scarcity."
~ John D. Vehr

The John Vehr in the quote above is a friend of mine and before I moved to Michigan he and I would have a monthly lunch together to talk about life, business, love, parenting, political outrage and whatever felt interesting.

Despite John's provocative views on a lot of popular issues his optimism is always shining through and his remarkable successes in the world of business tell you that he walks his talk and has skin in the game.

So what's the deal with that quote up above? What are we to make of that? Is it true? Does abundance exist everywhere? And when I experience scarcity, have I myself actually created it?

"Your thinking creates it," John says.

Let's set aside the issues of famine and poverty and social and political systems that have put people in situations where material and financial scarcity has become a physical reality. Some people have argued online with John's quote based on their looking at it through that lens of social justice.

I prefer to look at the quote from a personal lens. That way I can see how it applies to individual people like me. Let's take the quote personally. One example comes immediately to mind.

If I want to increase my income, there are people out there waiting to be helped and served right now. (Not at some future date when I get my act together, or when I become fortunate.)

Opportunities for serving people are out there in abundance.

When I couldn't see that reality I struggled financially because my thinking was always creating scarcity. It was making things look hard. It was making people look intimidating. It was pulling me down.

My thoughts of scarcity developed into a judgment cascade and then solidified into serious beliefs about personal limitations. I became a believer! I believed in my personal permanent characteristics, which unfortunately were weaknesses and shortcomings. Then those beliefs weighed me down further. I was drowning in debt. I started to think I was depressed. I was scaring myself.

All in my thinking.

Those images were blocking out reality. When I pulled a worried thought down and made it the truth it was exactly like pulling the shade down on my window and losing the light of the sun.

When I awoke to the possibility that lives inside John Vehr's reflection on abundance, everything changed. I saw that there were things I could do *right now* to connect my service to abundance. Once I saw that and took action on that insight I was able to help clients do the same.

The first step to overcoming an injustice
(righting a wrong, creating lasting change)
is the realization that your feelings
cannot be affected by it.

~ Garret Kramer

Waking People Up
to the Abundance

There was a community college in a state out West that hired me to help them deal with what they saw as an external, real-world problem.

They thought that in their state there was only so much money to go around and the major university down the highway was getting it all. The donations to the little community college were scarce and the donations flowing in to the big university looked abundant.

"We have a hard time raising money here because of who we are," the Director of Development told me when I arrived to consult with them. "We are a small college without connections to the kinds of people who make large donations."

That's what she thought.

Fortunately I had learned by then how fleeting and insubstantial any thought was. She was believing an arbitrary thought. Maybe that seems obvious from the vantage point of where you and I are right now. But it was the very insight that allowed me to help turn things around at that school. One thing led to another and soon we had larger and larger donations coming in to help that little community college.

If I had taken her thought to be actual solid reality, I would have had to try to help them go to war with that reality and see what kind of changes we could make to the prevailing negative circumstance.

We didn't do that, because it wasn't reality. It was virtual reality.

What we did instead was set those thoughts of scarcity aside so our minds could settle and be clear. Like a glass of muddy water, we allowed the dirt to settle and things got clear. Inspiration and creativity showed up inside that relaxed clarity and we began to see how we could serve donors.

My own history with scarcity thinking helped me. I had been a poster boy for Dr. Martin Seligman's studies on "learned helplessness." I had become like the singer in "Old Man River" who sings, "I get weary, and sick of trying, I'm tired of living and scared of dying."

The fundraisers at the little college were also weary. They were sick of trying to create abundance. They were tired of asking for money and yet scared that their school and their department might soon be dying.

My job was to show up as Old Man River himself. Someone who could show them that they could just keep rolling along. Let's sit down around this table and get the flow going. Let's stop focusing on us and start looking at our donors. Let's be open to the abundance that is already there.

The system they learned, of serving their donors instead of serving their own goals and needs, is a system I learned from Michael Bassoff, my co-author of the book *Relationshift: Revolutionary Fundraising*. Donors want to make a difference in the world. That's why they donate. And if you show them the exact difference their donation is making, and if you build strong and lasting relationships with them based on that, they will become more and more inspired to help.

So the development team watched as their thinking changed. They began to see that they were actually serving the donors by giving them a way to make a difference in life. They got to know their donors better and appreciate them more. Their relationships began to be built on gratitude and close collaboration. No longer were the donors seen as impersonal targets. No longer were donors "set up" for the next uncomfortable "ask." They were now seen as real people you could communicate with heart-to-heart, instead of distant, clueless, stingy people you had to give a dog and pony presentation to, or people you had to beg your own board members to "hit up" for small, reluctant donations.

Scarcity, for this little school, had been a thought posing as reality. It was a thought everyone agreed to believe. It spread through the college like a religion. And then it was gone.

Last night I dreamed I had no possessions,
and I nearly fainted from joy.

~ Rumi

And Now for the Word "Abundance" Itself

I hear the word "abundance" a lot on the internet and in the world of spiritual healing and personal growth. It is always talked about like it's obviously the best goal ever.

Some people I knew started to do meridian tapping for abundance, and if you look that up you can find a lot of sources that will teach it. You tap certain points on your body so that you can begin attracting money.

That kind of abundance, that seems to wait out there on a distant star, can become the dreamy goal of new-agers everywhere. People who begin saying, "I want it all!" And the vulgarity of that statement doesn't occur to them or stop them from desperately seeking their future treasure.

Moreover, if you don't call it money and you call it abundance it feels more spiritual.

But the true meaning of abundance is excess.

It means an over-sufficient supply of something. It means you have an overwhelming and unnecessarily plentiful amount of something. (You actually have enough to gag on.)

Imagine all the people praying for that! I want to gag,

Lord. Let me gag on material things.

Thinking that my scarcity feeling (caused by my scarcity thinking) can be eliminated only by my "creating" a *more than* sufficient, overwhelming and excessive amount of riches . . . enough to gag on . . . is tortured thinking. But it's probably a result of how painful it is to harbor and believe those scarcity thoughts. Sadly, it is a failure to recognize what is actually needed.

What is needed is known to most calm and secure people as "enough." Enough for a good life. Or enough for a community college to provide more and better education.

The future enters into us, in order to transform itself in us, long before it happens.

~ Rainer Maria Rilke

The Music in This Very Moment

Now I may not be an award-winning singer, but I can sing a song right now.

And just as William James said, "I don't sing because I'm happy; I'm happy because I sing."

And I may not be a talented dancer but I can get up and sway to the music this very moment.

And I may not be a great romancer but I can write someone a love letter and send them a flower the minute I finish this sentence.

But what if I have patterns of failed attempts at things? What if I have started previous projects and quit? What does that say about me?

If I am coaching you, it says nothing about you. So I will answer those questions with another question: What do you want to make of this moment together?

What if you saw that the past does not create the present? What if you could see that the present is what creates the past? It creates everything. It even creates the future.

Or, at least that is what seems to be my experience. And I want to base everything I say here on experience. I can trust that.

Which isn't the same thing as trusting myself. (My smaller personal self.)

People used to tell me, "Trust yourself!" And that was hard to do once I saw that I had made myself up. It was as if I had played the Phantom in a musical and out in real life, off-stage people kept saying to me, "Learn to trust the Phantom!" How could I if I knew I wasn't really the Phantom?

No, it's stronger to just trust my experience.

You ask about your past patterns and it's 'my experience that your patterns don't have to matter. You only make them matter when you believe that they are significant . . . when you believe that past patterns can cause behavior.

The patterns you perceive aren't the cause of behavior; they are the result of behavior.

So you can write them off as past history. Maybe interesting, maybe not. But merely history. And if you're willing to see them as past history, you and I can meet each other right here right now in the present moment. From here we can create a brand-new past and a brand-new future.

Remember then: there is only one time that is important—*Now*! It is the most important time because it is the only time when we have any *power*.

~ **Leo Tolstoy**

What If This Were My Only Job?

In an interview he recently gave to *The Tennessean* country star Keith Urban said that if he starts to feel disconnected from his audience during a concert he stops, takes a drink of water, and comes back to full attention.

"I do whatever I have to do to get back to being completely in the moment," Urban said. "Otherwise I might as well be at home. My only job is to be in the moment."

What if we all had that realization? That our only job was to be in the moment?

In a sermon he gave in 1931 John Haynes Holmes recalled meeting Mahatma Gandhi: "I stepped into the little cabin. Instantly, Gandhi jumped to his feet, and, with the lithe, quick step of a school-boy, came forward to greet me. I felt his hands take mine in a grasp as firm as that of an athlete. I saw his eyes shining with a light so bright that not even the thick glass of his rude spectacles could obscure their radiance. I heard his voice addressing me in tones as rich and full as they were gentle. We had a few precious moments together. I was confused and excited, and today have little memory of what was said."

Contrast Holmes' experience to the guy you met with

today who seemed like he wasn't even there. He was making repeated glances at his phone as text signals beeped, and his unfocused eyes made little contact with yours. His eyes were alternately clouded over with images of the future he wanted to be in, or the past he was now regretting.

Later he would wish he had a better relationship with you. If he tried to figure out why he didn't he'd either conclude that there was something wrong with his personality or yours. He wouldn't see that he was *never there* when you two met. How can you have a great relationship with someone who isn't there?

The world is but a canvas
to the imagination.

~ **Henry David Thoreau**

What's the Name of That Actor?

You're trying to think of his name. You know, that actor! He was in that movie with Jennifer Lawrence. He's in a TV series now. You try and try to think of his name but you just can't.

So you drop the whole thing, and you decide to carry some dishes to the sink in the kitchen. You start to scrape and rinse the dishes and then BOOM! The name appears!

What just happened?

You were trying to utilize highly-controlled personal thinking to access something that comes from somewhere else. This will happen any time you try desperately to figure something out. You keep feeding it into the cyclotron of your neocortex and it whirls faster and faster, colliding with other particles of thought. But the answer is never there.

The answer comes from somewhere else. It comes when the grip is relaxed.

Here's an even more important example.

You're writing something creative, say a book or a song or a blog, and you keep trying to figure out the next lyric or line. You think and you think and you pace and you fret. After you give up writing for the day you step into the shower and BOOM! the idea flies in.

The grip was released.

And we start to understand that creativity and inspiration do not flow into a mind that grips and clenches.

I can release my death grip and drop out of my whirling thinking. Dropping out of my personal thinking is like telling my inner editor to take a hike. I will call on him later. If I'm letting him judge my writing as it is happening the flow stops.

The Dalai Lama keeps teaching that when there is no judgment we fall in love. Without that judgment, love is all there is. When I stopped judging the garbage as a dreary, boring chore, I fell in love with doing it. I had slowed it down to the speed of the present moment. I gave myself a chance to experience the *beauty* of the present moment.

It's the same thing as dropping into the now. I don't force my way into the now. I don't achieve the now. I don't "deserve" the now because of my efforts. I fall. Just as I don't deserve or achieve the love I feel when I fall in love. I just fall.

When I do that my creativity is unlimited. It is not governed by my personal history. It does not pay any attention to whether I think I am "a creative person" or not.

Compassion isn't about solutions.
It's about giving all the love that you've got.

~ **Cheryl Strayed**

Those Who Can, Do;
Those Who Can't, Teach

That biting little piece of wisdom is repeated by a lot of people because it sounds so clever and insightful. It is meant to make a mockery of teachers and make them look inauthentic.

I have the highest respect for people who teach things and I think in most cases their positive influence spreads out through the whole world. Further than they ever realize.

But despite the mean spirit there's some encouraging truth in that saying.

People who succeed quickly in their field seldom turn out to be the best teachers. Nor are they the best coaches in sports and the arts.

Watching the great basketball star Larry Bird trying to coach a basketball team was fascinating. I could see his frustration. When his players messed up, he just couldn't understand it. He paced the sidelines in a state of confusion and exasperation. How could they not know what to do? The frustration became intolerable and he finally got out of coaching.

The best coaches were not great players like Larry Bird. So they know what it is to struggle and fail and learn the game slowly. That's why they are such wise and skilled teachers.

In his delightful and inspiring TED Talk (check it out— it's called "Why Aren't We Awesomer?") my friend Michael Neill talks about his days of suicidal depression. Today Michael is an amazingly successful coach and author. So much better at coaching than someone who always had his act together.

Contrast his remarkable track record for helping people with that of another coach I know, one who struggles at his chosen coaching practice. He thought coaching would be a piece of cake, given how successful he was in business. I'll call that person Buzz. I call him that because he comes across like the *Toy Story* character Buzz Lightyear.

His life has been a series of financial successes and so Buzz believes everyone will want to learn from him. I watch him talk to a group of people and he is speaking with a booming voice, smiling constantly between sentences as if he were selling luxury vehicles. Buzz gets confused when his clients don't take his excellent advice to just "go out there and crush it!" His attempts to enroll people into his practice fall flat and he can't understand why his "closing ratio" is low.

He doesn't see that people are having a hard time relating to him. His efforts to demonstrate his superiority are distancing him from the people he wants money from. He's just too perfect. He's Larry Bird trying to be a coach. Clients and potential clients can feel (or imagine) his judgment of them right away. He has no understanding of why they feel put off.

Buzz can't see that an effective coach levels the playing field with the client. His or her first objective is to settle the client down and create a conversation that feels like two average people helping each other out. Right here and right now. Not a conversation that focuses on the past accomplishments of the coach.

I remember the day one of my own coaches told me about struggles he had. They were real and dramatic. He had been wild and criminally destructive. He drank himself into a coma. He sank into a near suicidal depression.

From that moment on I trusted his every word. I saw that he was, at the heart of it, just like me.

Compassion is the key to all this. Slowing down and listening deeply and understanding and identifying with another person. Leaving the past and the future out of the experience and connecting in this present moment.

When grief and loss and sorrow wash through us unimpeded and without judgment we experience these feelings as the natural and beautiful flow of life.

~ **Dicken Bettinger**

Breathe Back into the Here and Now

When a baseball coach or manager walks out to the mound to talk to the pitcher it's usually not the advice he's going to give that's most valuable in that moment.

But as we watch from the stands we think it must be! We imagine he's going to tell the pitcher what strategy to use against the next batter.

Maybe the pitcher had just given up a home run and then, feeling rattled and upset with himself, he's walked the next two batters.

What the coach really does by walking out there and chatting with the pitcher is settle the pitcher down . . . in other words, he gets him back into the present moment. They might not even be talking about baseball. Because the good thing that is happening is that the pitcher is starting to *breathe normally* again. And with those relaxed breaths, the pitcher is restored to his normal workaday feel for the game. His balance is back. His true talent and skills have returned to him as his mind clears.

We watch as he is throwing strikes again.

We think it must be the strategy. But in fact he's just settled down. He's no longer trying to overcome his past or force his way into a better future. He has returned his activity to one pitch at a time. This pitch right here. This pitch right now.

Feelings come and go like clouds in a windy sky.
Conscious breathing is my anchor.

~ **Thich Nhat Hanh**

What Makes You Feel This Way?

Do you think like a victim? Do you take things personally?

If so, join the club. I did for decades.

And it wasn't because of a character flaw or a pathological personality defect (as much as I thought it was). I was simply unaware that I didn't have to give credibility to my victim thoughts. I didn't have to follow them all the way down the rabbit hole, holding on for dear life all the way down.

In the past I always gave each successive negative thought a lot of depth and weight. I was letting each thought bring in clusters of related and equally discouraging thoughts.

But once the awareness checked in . . . the awareness that I could just let it go . . . it isn't true reality . . . it is just a thought! . . . my life changed for the better.

From that point on I defined ownership as taking whatever life gives you and welcoming it in. Owning it. I defined the victim thought cluster as one that sees circumstance as all powerful . . . and often those circumstances look negative and emotionally overwhelming.

I first got the idea for my victim thinking seminars from the many books I'd read by British philosopher Colin Wilson, whose philosophy was that humans have an endless innate capacity for optimism and creativity already built in. However, they bypass and ignore that resource in favor of the mistaken pessimistic viewpoint that life is difficult and oppressive. When we live long enough in that viewpoint we humans become weak and miserable.

Wilson said we could drop the pessimism in a heartbeat the moment we understood the depth of our untapped resources.

Wilson's optimistic philosophy struck a chord with me and the more I understood it, the more I experienced it to be true. When I believed my victim thoughts it felt like life was presenting me with a series of difficult situations I had to learn to "get through." But when I chose to believe my ownership thoughts (thereby acknowledging ownership of my built-in, powerful human spirit) I saw the same situations as opportunities for learning. I went from "get through" to "get from."

Organizations who took the training also woke up to their previously unrecognized power to create and innovate and bring good energy to everything they encountered. They started to ask what they could "get from" any situation that used to be automatically thought of as another problem to "get through."

One reason the training clicked and became useful was because it was allowing people to see the true origin of their victimized feelings. Those feelings were not caused by the situation itself, but rather by the way they were thinking about it.

So the real difference between the owner (of their inner unlimited human spirit) and the victim was that the owner realized that situations by themselves could not cause morale or energy to deflate. It was always just the thought. And you didn't have to go with your first thought about anything.

Colin Wilson put it best when he wrote, "When I open my eyes in the morning I am not confronted by a world, but by a million possible worlds."

It is not an easy thing for people to see what Wilson saw . . . that we live in a thought-projected world of infinite possibility. They just assume that we live in one real, external world, and that that world is a consistent challenge. They have been conditioned to believe that circumstances and other people are the cause of what they feel.

So they feel zapped by others, and zapped by fate, and zapped by this and zapped by that and no wonder life becomes hard to live. They are like flies flying into one of those electronic insect zappers. Who's not going to buckle under all that zapping? Who's going to wake up into that world singing, "Oh, what a beautiful morning!"?

We have been heavily conditioned by culture and society to interpret our feelings this way. We learn at an early age that they come from outside sources. People who loved us kept telling us they hoped something good would "happen" to us. The thought was that something would come from the outside world and envelop us with its inherent goodness!

People referred to those good things happening as "being blessed." If something came along, a new romantic mate, a job offer, a newborn child, a good day at the race track, they would say, "I've been blessed."

It didn't occur to them that the biggest blessing of all, dwarfing all those outside happenings, was consciousness itself. What they wake up into each day. The true miracle of present moment awareness. That inner, seemingly empty resource that is actually pregnant with optimism and creativity.

That's the ultimate blessing right there.

If I believe blessings must be bestowed in the form of good outside circumstances, then no wonder the outside world seems to contain all the power over my feelings. It feels like one day I could be blessed by life, and the next day cursed by life. Truly an anxiety-producing set up. Could that really be how life works?

Like Alan Watts used to say, if you were God would you create life so that it worked that way? Not if you were God. No way.

Don't take anything personally. Nothing others do is because of you.

~ Don Miguel Ruiz

She's Heavier Now but She'll Still Tweet

I saw in a news item that a certain famous singer tweeted out that she was gaining weight because a political election didn't go the way she wanted it to go. The candidate she had been opposed to was causing her to sulk and eat pancakes.

"I have been gorging on pancakes ever since he was elected," she said, and she reported that her weight was skyrocketing.

The implication was that if the election had gone the other way (an obvious blessing that didn't occur), she'd be slim and trim. She might be serenely eating raw kale and sipping cucumber water while her weight went down.

But unfortunately that outside world event didn't happen, and so she was gaining weight. How else do you counter-balance such a curse?

If she were my coaching client we might start our work by exploring a question I never thought I'd ever get to ask anyone: "Can another person cause you to eat pancakes?"

Contrast that singer's newly-bloated predicament with another woman I know who also disliked the outcome of that same election. She saw that her feelings of disappointment were only a result of her own thinking and she let those thoughts pass. She then jumped into action and formed a powerful group of people who would take actions to impact her community in ways that would make a positive difference and counter what she thought was politically off-base in the newly-elected candidate's programs.

She was out in the world making a difference right now while our favorite singer was sitting at home helplessly eating pancakes.

Of course our pop star is innocent in her misunderstanding. She is living out what she has learned from a very young age. She would have gotten the message from her family, society, the media and the culture: We are all either the beneficiaries of or the victims of circumstance.

And then it begins to feel like we are most often the victims, as expressed in the phrase, "That's life!" That phrase is only used when something bad happens, and so it suggests that life itself, by its very nature, trends that way.

Our popular singer might be listening to classic Frank Sinatra as she reaches for the syrup. Yes, he's singing "That's Life," all about "riding high in April, shot down in May." And in his hit song "The Curse of an Aching Heart" he sings "You made me what I am today, I hope you're satisfied. You dragged and dragged me down until the soul within me died."

That's a view of how our minds and hearts function that is simply mistaken. And fortunately we are pulling out of this misunderstanding.

Colin Wilson was before his time in pointing out this pessimistic error, and the intellectual literary critics savaged his work in the same way that Galileo was savaged by the Catholic Church for daring to discover that the Earth was not the center of the solar system, and that the sun did not actually rise in the east and set in the west. It just looked that way. It was the classic error of confusing causation with visual correlation.

Our own thoughts produce our feelings. That's not some kind of self-help theory or affirmation. It's how the human system works. It's how the universe is actually rolling. Learning this is like learning true astronomy instead of the old superstitious astrology.

So if I rise and think "Oh, what a beautiful morning, oh, what a beautiful day" it's those two thoughts that cause my good feelings. I might not have even looked out the window yet!

If you surrender completely to the moments
as they pass, you live more richly
those moments.

~ **Anne Morrow Lindbergh**

What If a Disadvantage Didn't Matter?

The mother of my four children had a brain disorder developed in the midst of childhood trauma and abuse.

We didn't know it was there and for a number of years things were fine at home and there was no hint of what was to come. But one day, during a psychological program she was participating in, she had what we used to call a nervous breakdown. One doctor told me it was a "psychotic break from reality" and said she would never be the same. Another psychologist said it was a "post-traumatic event" that arose after years of successful memory repression.

Whatever it was, it took her away from us. She went into an institution for long-term treatment. The children were young; the youngest was three and the oldest was twelve. I was soon given full custody of them and the civil court judge wished me luck.

My clearest memory from those dramatic days was one morning after the children's mother had been gone for a couple weeks and the reality had hit them that she might never return to them. I was afraid for them. I wondered if they might now be traumatized by this scary turn of events.

On that one morning, though, something strange occurred. As I woke up in my bed I heard some banging and yelling way down the hall in the far side of the house. (We lived in a ranch-style house in Tucson and the family room was way across the house and down a distant hall from my bedroom.)

It took me a few minutes to understand what this noise was. Was someone hitting a pot or a pan with a spoon? It sounded like it. Were the children chanting something? I sat up in bed and then I got what was happening.

My children's (and my) favorite movie at that time was *Meatballs*, starring Bill Murray. (And if you watch it, just watch the original, not the sequels.) There's a defining moment in the movie when summer-camp counselor Bill Murray is giving a pep talk to his kids, who are a ragtag bunch from the poor side of town. Bill's kids are resting at half time of an Olympic-style competition against the camp across the lake, and they are losing. The camp across the lake is a private camp filled with children of the wealthy, and in the movie the rich kids are arrogant and dismissive of their opponents. Bill gathers his campers together and tells them that the kids across the lake have all the advantages and perks of being wealthy and privileged. The kids start to look even more downhearted and confused until Bill says, "But it just doesn't matter!" The kids look up, surprised and he keeps going.

Bill screams, "It just doesn't matter! We could win or we could lose and it wouldn't matter BECAUSE ALL THE GOOD-LOOKING GIRLS WOULD STILL GO OUT WITH THE CAMP MOHAWK GUYS BECAUSE THEY HAVE ALL THE MONEY!!!!" And the kids start laughing and picking up the chant, "We could win or we could lose BUT IT JUST DOESN'T MATTER!" Soon they are chanting "It just doesn't matter!" over and over. It was my kids' favorite scene in the movie and it was what I was hearing from them down the hall.

One of my kids would yell out, "Our mother was taken away from us" and they all would chant in reply, "But it just doesn't matter, it just doesn't matter!" I heard one yell, "Our father doesn't know what he's doing!" and then, "But it just doesn't matter, it just doesn't matter!"

I was filled with amazed good feelings in that moment because I knew right then that we'd be okay. We'd always be okay. There was crazy love in this house, and in the face of that, circumstance had no power. And more than that, we had humor. Maybe this would be, after all, a not-so-serious life. And maybe we could love that.

The children are grown now, and we often get together and laugh about those days . . . those days that easily could have been labeled as tragic. We could have covered ourselves in that label and most people would give us a nod of deep, sorrowful understanding.

Sometimes today when people hear I had full custody of four children all those years their faces grow sad and I can see they are feeling sorry for me. When I tell them it was a great adventure and that I learned so much from my children they think I'm giving it the ever-popular re-frame. I imagine some think I'm a self-help writer and a motivational speaker and I need to always try to come across as a positive, enlightened being to people in support of my personal brand. But it was just the truth.

It's hard to explain how true it was. I was a father who didn't know what he was doing, and it just didn't matter.

And as far as being happy and still enjoying life, we could forget the past and not worry about the future. In this moment, banging on these pots, marching around the house, we have entered the present moment. So the past and the future? They just didn't matter.

The pursuit of truth and beauty is a sphere of activity in which we are permitted to remain children all our lives.

~ **Albert Einstein**

Who Are My Real Teachers in Life?

It often sounds idiotic to me when someone says they are learning things from their children.

When I'm in a bad mood I wonder if there's some dysfunctional role-reversal happening in that household when I hear that. When people say in a saintly voice, "My children are my teachers," I gag. I think, "Oh isn't that just so precious . . . another attempt to show the world how wise and progressive you are. Damn it, wake up and grow up! Children are supposed to be learning from *you*!"

But when I come to my senses I can see something else. I can see that children have a connection to an inner something, maybe an inner resilience and an inner wisdom about the humor of life, the joy of life, that we adults have been systematically disconnecting from. Our lives have been a serial disconnection from that. It's as if we grown-ups have been walking around the house and one-by-one pulling out all the electrical plugs from the walls so that the house keeps getting darker and darker.

But why would we do that?

Why would we knowingly disconnect from our power to enjoy life? Our power to chant and beat on pots and pans?

If I can temporarily eliminate all of life's distractions, I can start to see the answer to that. If I take a clear look at my own serial disconnection, I can see it even more clearly. When I explore the question, "Why would I knowingly disconnect from my power to enjoy life?" the key word becomes "knowingly." That has to be the answer as to why it happens:

I don't know I'm doing it.

The trouble is,
you think
you have time.

~ Jack Kornfield

Disconnecting from the Source of Happiness

My own disconnection happened because I was gathering discouraging beliefs as I got older. They were negative and pessimistic beliefs that soon became heavy in my heart like stones.

They were heavy like the stones that Virginia Woolf filled her pockets with on the 28th of March in 1941 before she wandered into the water to drown herself. That kind of heavy.

The older I got the more I was walking the earth filled with many cold stones of belief.

It wasn't until my coach introduced me to the work of Byron Katie that I began to understand why he'd ask this powerful question: "What are you believing about yourself that would cause you to feel the way you do?"

That's where feelings come from? Our thoughts?

I was feeling discouraged, defeated and, as my mother used to put it, "down in the dumps." And I would point to situations and circumstances that I thought were causing those feelings. And then my coach would guide me back inside to look for the belief. And that always turned out to be the answer.

Or, as Byron Katie likes to ask, "What is the thought that kicks you out of heaven?"

Once I really heard that question, it became the most useful question in the world to me. I began to use that question with myself and my clients. I even do an exercise in my seminars where I put a volunteer up on a stool in front of the room and simply ask that question, "What is the thought that kicks you out of heaven?" and we take it from there.

After doing that enough times, more and more light comes in. It becomes a great unraveling. It is an effective way to deconstruct and disentangle a negative belief system. It's an opportunity to start fresh right then and there in the beauty of the present moment, seeing the role of thought.

Without thought and belief, there is nothing left but truth. And truth is beauty. As the poet John Keats wrote, "Beauty is truth, truth beauty, —that is all ye know on earth, and all ye need to know."

Beautiful moments occur up on that chair in front of the room. We originally called it "the hot seat" to acknowledge the courage of the people who volunteered to sit there and do the inquiry. Later it got the name "The Clarity Chair" because of the head-clearing truth that kept arising from the exercise.

We are asleep
With compasses in our hands.

~ W.S. Merwin

So Sad it Became Funny

It would be puzzling if we actually disconnected from our inner fire *knowingly*. If we woke up and deliberately chose to spend the day toggling back and forth between a badly-remembered past and a completely fantasized future, all the while losing energy and hope.

But once I saw that I was doing that, I started asking myself some questions. Is my memory of my past accurate? Did my father really never believe in me? For years I crafted resentments from fleeting, faded memories. I had begun thinking I was never given enough encouragement to have good survival skills. I started picturing worst-case scenarios for the future. I saw myself as a homeless person.

I heard an interview with Larry David (the major writer for the *Seinfeld* TV series) once in which he said he had such vivid fears of ending up homeless that he'd actually picked out a spot on the street for himself.

He discovered humor to be his road to freedom from all this illusion.

Sometimes being funny can be a way to bring the truth in. To realize what the sages and mystics of old meant when they said that enlightenment was "the restoration of humor" to human life. (Notice how many times a day children laugh.)

My friend and colleague Jason Goldberg and I created a little internet show called *The Not-So-Serious Life* as a playful experiment that explored the potential of lightheartedness. We had viewers send us real-life questions about real-life problems, and although we didn't try to dismiss the pain that (thinking about) these problems had produced for our people, we had fun offering creative solutions and enjoying the challenge of the problems. We were playing with solutions instead of desperately seeking them. (You can see these episodes on YouTube and other places on the internet.) And although some critics said we were taking people's problems too lightly, I've never regretted exploring the function of fun as a problem-solving system.

Another example of seeing how humor can open up a mind closed down by beliefs is in a short video done by Fred Knipe, as his comedic character Dr. Ludiker gives us advice on the subject of credentials. You'll find that on YouTube too. I've used it to help professional coaches and consultants who are stressed out about whether their credentials are impressive enough. They laugh when they see it and their hearts are suddenly lighter.

I've often wondered what would happen if you gave people an honest, real-life choice between humor and self-improvement. Let's say you had three theaters on a theater row and the first one had a religious figure who could lift you up spiritually and maybe even save your soul, and in the next theater you had a motivational guru who could give you great ideas for self-improvement, and in the third theater the funniest stand-up comic in the country. Where would the lines be the longest? I think it would be with the comedian.

And it wouldn't be just because people would rather be entertained than improved or spiritually saved. I think it would be because something deeper calls them to the humor. We secretly know that there is something explosive and non-linear about humor that can open us up in a heartbeat. Instant freedom from our thinking. Whereas those other disciplines can take lifetimes of practice. (And there is still no guarantee of freedom.)

A laugh is a spontaneous opening. It instantly opens even the most tightly-closed mind. It's a burst of childhood happiness that blows the confetti of your serious thoughts back out into space. It's a bodily eruption of total surprise. An unexpected and irresistible surge of joy in the line, a power surge that can momentarily shut down your analytical biocomputer altogether!

Even on a biological level the flood of endorphins that comes from laughter is proven to be healing. A good joke stops you from taking your previous thinking seriously.

So the next time you have a serious problem that you are bringing to your coach to solve you might get your best result by saying, "Help me have some fun with this."

Life is a tragedy when seen in close-up, but a comedy in long-shot.

~ **Charlie Chaplin**

Let Me Ask You a Question

My friend and mentor, educational psychologist Dr. Dicken Bettinger (author of *Coming Home*), told me about a question he had been pondering for a while.

It was a question about being "in the now"—about being fully surrendered into the present moment. (Surrendering, as in allowing yourself to fall.)

He was wondering, "Can you be in the now and not be happy?"

At first I thought yes, of course you can. For example, I could be sitting in the waiting room waiting for an outpatient procedure at a clinic and be "in the now" and not be happy.

And then I looked more clearly at that scenario and realized that I would not really be in the now. I'd be lost in thinking about the immediate future: *How painful is this going to be?* Then my thoughts would be in the past: *How long have I been waiting?* Then back to the future: *How long will this thing take?*

My mind would become a particle accelerator. Whirling particles of thought about the past and my negative imaginary future.

Then I pictured myself face to face with a large bear in the woods. I would certainly be in the now in that moment. I would not be mentally making dinner plans (like the bear would be doing). But the more I looked at it the more I saw that the fear that would be freezing me would be coming from a thought about the future, picturing what might happen to me.

So I kept trying to come up with other times when I was completely in the now, and each time I saw myself as happy. I'm not saying I won't succeed in finding a time when I'm in the now and not happy. I'm willing to keep trying.

But so far each fully in-the-now experience I can find is a happy one. Maybe it's because they are synonymous. Being happy and being in-the-now are the same thing. Aren't they? It's a great feeling being here in the present moment. When I'm happy like this there's no place I would rather go.

The Beatles song lyric floats through my mind, "But oh, that magic feeling, nowhere to go."

What is now proved was
once only imagined.

~ William Blake

He Never Finishes Anything

Levon is the name I will give to a person who hired me to help him with a debilitating problem.

He admitted that he didn't know if I could help him solve this thing, given his long history with it, but he was willing to try anything. He called me at our appointed early morning coaching hour, and I asked him what the problem was.

"I never finish anything," he said.

I asked him to talk more about that and he told me it ran through his whole life and it caused him all sorts of problems with his wife and family and he was really discouraged and down on himself.

I decided to ask him some unusual questions. I thought I might find an opening in the way he saw the world.

I knew Levon was a dedicated outdoorsman so I asked him what kind of shoes he was wearing. Just as I'd hoped, he said he was wearing hiking boots.

I said, "Are they the kind you have to tie? Do they have laces?"

"Yes, of course. Are there hiking boots that don't?"

I had to admit that I wouldn't know that. But I continued

by saying, "Are they tied right now, all the way up?"

"Yes."

"And this morning when you put them on, were they tied? Were they tied before you put them on?"

Levon said, "No," and I could hear that he was getting impatient.

"Okay, good, so you put them on, and then you started to tie them and then you finished tying them. So that's something you started and finished."

"Well, yeah, but . . ."

I said, "Did you finish high school?"

There was a pause and then he said yes.

I said, "Oh good, so you started high school and you went all the way through high school and you finished high school."

"Right," he said.

I told him that was another thing right there that he started and finished and not to think it was a minor thing. I'd read an article that said over 45 percent of students in Los Angeles County don't finish high school. They start but they don't finish.

And there are a lot of people who sit around the house with their laces untied.

We inquired about three or four more things in his world, all of which he had finished. Soon he'd had enough.

"I don't see where you're going with all this," he said. "These things that I did finish are not that big a deal. Well, maybe high school, but . . ."

I said I understood that, but I wanted to make the point that if we inquired long enough we'd also find a lot of things that were very important to him that he did finish, and that my point was to show him that his belief—"I never finish anything"—was not true.

"You finish almost everything," I said.

He was silent but he didn't disagree.

So we talked about the consequences of living in a world of falsehood. A world of labels. What exactly happens to someone who finishes almost everything but then they see the world, and themselves, through the filter of "I never finish anything"?

Levon said he wasn't sure what happens to those people.

"They end up like you!" I said.

He tried to laugh.

I told him that when someone walks around believing something false and disrespectful about themselves they limit their capacity to love life and take action. Who would want that? They get bogged down in a false identity that they think *explains* their behavior. Even produces it! So just as Kevin Costner's character in the movie had the Indian name "Dances With Wolves," Levon now walked around his house with the identity, "Never Finishes Anything." Imagine that his family sees him come into the room and they cheerfully cry out, "Oh look, here comes Never Finishes Anything!" At least that's how it feels. And when you feel like that it gets harder and harder to finish things.

He was seeing it. It began to look funny to him. But I knew we hadn't addressed the problem behind the problem . . . the actual reason he was calling this a problem. So I asked him what was it, specifically, that he hadn't finished that was the focus of his downhearted thinking.

"The basement game room," he said. "I started painting it a year ago, but it was such a big project I had to postpone work on it and I've never gotten back to it and my wife keeps bringing it up."

I told Levon that one of my biggest epiphanies ever was realizing that there were always things I could do right now. Things that didn't have to wait. And if he was willing, I'd be an accountability partner for him in painting this basement right now. But it was up to him.

He said he would love that.

For the next two weeks Levon sent me phone pics of the painting progress in his basement and, as we'd agreed to, he was completely finished with it by our next phone call.

Levon saw himself in a different light. He understood that his thinking was the only thing that was getting in his way. He got the difference between "I never finish anything" and "There's a basement that hasn't been finished." The first thought pulled Levon into a feeling of being personally defective. It disempowered him every time he believed it. And it wasn't even true. The second thought was just a neutral observation about the basement and an opportunity for action.

Colin Wilson once observed that if people saw life for what it really was—pure and endless opportunity—pessimism would become "a laughable absurdity."

If you accept a limiting belief,
then it will become a truth for you.

~ **Louise Hay**

Let Me Write That Book

Someday I want to write a book called *Self-Esteem for Dummies*. When I told my friend Jason Goldberg about it he said it would be interesting to observe how many times people would pull it down from the shelf and quickly put it back again.

When Colin Wilson writes about his own life he says that his self-esteem as a teenager hit a dangerous low. There was a moment in his teenage years when he was about to commit suicide by swallowing hydrocyanic acid.

Just before doing it he was shaken awake by a new thought. The thought told him that an "idiotic, self-pitying teenager" was about to kill the real Colin Wilson, that higher Self that needs no worldly esteem or self-esteem.

"In that moment," he wrote in his autobiography *Dreaming to Some Purpose*, "I glimpsed the marvelous, immense richness of reality, extending to distant horizons."

From that point on, he went on to energetically, joyfully write over a hundred books. He didn't even much care that he incurred the relentless criticism of intellectuals and reviewers who thought that this working-class "philosopher" hadn't paid his academic dues and was a fool to criticize the eloquent and delicately nuanced pessimism of such giants as

Jean-Paul Sartre and Albert Camus.

When essayist Robert Meadley published a defense of Wilson called *The Odyssey of a Dogged Optimist*, he pointed out that newspapers and journals were protesting Wilson's philosophy a bit too much. He marveled at the huge amount of space they were giving their criticisms of Wilson. Meadley wrote, "If you think a man's a fool, and his books are a waste of time, how long does it take to say so?"

Push-back and knee-jerk criticism is what can happen when you challenge people's long-held victim stories about "the human condition"—a phrase that suggests that being human is a kind of disease for which there isn't much of a cure.

Wilson had a revelation in that post-suicidal moment when he saw the richness of life "extending to distant horizons." He realized that his life was not trapped inside the web of a tightly-crafted, egoic persona or separate self. His breakthrough was similar to the experiences of so many people who give their own accounts of near-death experiences.

It reminds me of the time I was asked to do a workshop for nurses who worked in a cancer hospital in Arizona. I decided to talk to a number of the nurses prior to my workshop to get some background information. I assumed that their work must be stressful, if not downright depressing, given that they worked with so many terminal patients.

They told me it was the opposite.

They said that a high percentage of their terminal patients, after passing through the initial acceptance of their prognosis, started seeing life differently. They began appreciating every day as a precious gift. They started to cherish and savor being alive. They were showing the nurses the peace and pleasure of living life inside the present moment. Living in the now was an inspiration to the nurses and they were grateful for the work they got to do.

In the past we made a pact with
the darkness; now our task
is to interpret the light.

~ **Pablo Neruda**

Does Self-Esteem
Have to Be Earned?

In the old psychological theories, self-esteem and self-confidence were something you either had built up or else you didn't have them. And if you didn't have them, you'd better learn to develop them!

They were identifiable outcomes. They were also sought-after labels. For example, "high self-esteem" was a label we would hope to stick on ourselves after steaming off the "low self-esteem" label.

But Dicken Bettinger has a more optimistic view of this subject. For me, he has been a master at interpreting the light.

In an interview with Sebastian Eck (available on YouTube) Dicken explains his viewpoint. It's based on decades of experience counseling young people and grown-ups (like me) on the true nature of psychological well-being.

As for self-esteem and self-confidence?

"We're born with them," he says.

They emerge, not from heroic practice and personal development, but whenever we drop out of our insecure thoughts, worries and judgments. There they are: self-confidence and self-esteem. They have been there all along.

When people feel anxious and uncertain for a period of time, that feeling gets labeled as low self-esteem. It becomes a condition you think you have. A condition that you might want to have fixed and corrected.

"We think that if somebody has a feeling of insecurity for a long time, that must be their true nature," Dicken says. "So we'll say, 'They don't have self-esteem.'"

But what's really occurring is that the person is feeling low as a result of their passing thoughts and the temporary feelings they create. Nothing worthy of a permanent label.

Dicken says that when those thoughts drop away, "that's what we would call *living in the now*. Anybody who is living in the now, free of worries and judgments, is going to have perfect self-esteem and self-confidence."

So it occurred to me that self-esteem actually looks a little like Kansas.

Dorothy asked Glinda the good witch how she could get back to Kansas and the good witch laughed because she knew Dorothy *was already there*. Oz was a dream. If she just clicked her heels she would wake up.

Dorothy had obviously been dreaming. But we are dreaming too when we see the world (and ourselves!) as projections of our insecure thoughts and beliefs.

Like waking up
From the longest dream
How real it seemed
Until your love broke through.

~ Keith Green and Randy Stonehill
Love Broke Through

Like Waking Up from
My Longest Dream

My longest dream was not a good dream. It truly was the dream of low self-esteem.

But my life didn't start that way.

Because I remember when I was three years old, running with absolute abandon across a yard of green grass and feeling like I owned the world . . . I *was* the world in that moment. No problem with low self-esteem because I was living in the moment and loving life.

In my adult years so many beliefs clouded my connection with life that the love that lived inside felt like it had to *break through* those beliefs to be fully felt and expressed.

That predicament comes from confusing a negative belief with the truth, and from confusing virtual reality (a thought) with true reality.

I tell myself, "My father doesn't trust me or believe in me," and now his facial expressions look like suspicion, when in fact they were neutral. His encouraging words, "You can do better," sound like hurtful criticism. Because they are being perceived through the lens of my beliefs. If I put on purple sunglasses everything looks purple, even the rain. If I put on beliefs of any color, the world and my father look like they *are* that color.

One day Dicken Bettinger told me he had been reading and enjoying *The Magic of Awareness* by Anam Thubten. I bought the book and devoured it. Then I took it everywhere with me for a month or so, like a kind of battery pack that I might need at any moment if my spirit lost its charge.

Anam Thubten is one of the rising Buddhist teachers in the West. He grew up in Tibet and began at an early age to practice in the Nyingma tradition of Tibetan Buddhism.

I underlined my book where Thubten wrote, ". . . everything we want to transcend doesn't really exist in the ultimate sense. It only exists as our own mind's display . . ."

If I'm displaying from my mind a wife who doesn't like me she can say, "You look good today" and my mind will translate it to mean, "You look good for a change."

My answer to her of "What's been wrong with the way I *have been* looking?" confuses her. She doesn't realize that I'm seeing through a faulty lens . . . the lens of my thinking.

I could have lived forever believing that my father didn't believe in me, but when I saw that this was just a projection from my own mind, life got open and bright.

Now the trick would be to find out how to transcend the filters. How to ditch the purple glasses. How to see and hear clearly. How to enjoy the whole of life *right now*.

When I look inside Thubten's *The Magic of Awareness* I see that he prescribes something he calls "crazy love."

"Crazy love is a very ecstatic way of transcending this mind and its ultimate mistake of buying into its own display," he says. "We just see everything as sacred and love everything without having any specific object of love . . . Love without boundaries, crazy love, is sacred perception . . . Crazy love loves everything . . ."

Wow. To me that sounds a little crazy. Maybe he knew it would sound that way, which is why he gave it the name. But when I read that I was willing to try it. I mean, I'll try anything. Wouldn't you? If it meant transcending the mind's projections?

Okay, so where to start? I looked back at the book and saw that Anam Thubten had anticipated my question.

He says, "The question is how do we, in this very ordinary moment, jump into that realm of crazy love? Instead of holding an answer as a kind of recipe, let's keep asking the question . . ."

He's brilliant. The answer won't be useful. Because his answer might not be mine. Mine might not be yours. So it's the question itself that I want to keep with me. How do I, in this very ordinary moment, jump into the realm of crazy love?

One of the great problems of history is that the concepts of love and power have usually been contrasted as opposites, so that love is identified with a resignation of power, and power with a denial of love.

~ Martin Luther King

Dead Leaves in My Pockets

Dead leaves. That's how I regard any bad memories I might have blowing through my mind today.

That was not true in the past. With eager encouragement from my psychotherapist I was asked to bring those memories back and give them fresh life and then experience the feelings that came up from that. It was suggested that we would "get it completed and out of your system."

So something you focus on and repeat over and over is going to, as a result, have less of a presence in your life? Looking back on that theory, it's easy to question. But at the time I was willing to do anything.

So I was cheered on and taught to cultivate my rage and give it new life. Sometimes I thought I would die trying to do that. Instead of completing and "getting closure" on my past memories, it only gave them more significance. Instead of giving me new life it gave my rage new life.

My clients come to their life-coaching (and even business-coaching) with a lot of dead leaves in their pockets. Some clients bring them out to try to give them life again and try to understand them as the cause of their current dysfunction. (We've been taught to think we must *fix* anything not immaculate in the memory bin.)

But how could this dead leaf be the *cause* of some current emotional energy? Maybe that whole practice was backwards.

My best experiences with myself and those I try to help happen when we let the wind just blow those leaves through and away. So we can start fresh. In this moment, with this beautiful green tree of life.

The winds must come from somewhere
  when they blow,
There must be reason why the leaves decay;
Time will say nothing but I told you so.

~ W.H. Auden

You and Your Fear of Success

Being in this coaching business I often run into people who claim to have a strange affliction called "fear of success." I actually have people tell me, with a straight face, that that is one of their major fears.

The problem is that there is no such thing. There is no such fear.

Why would there be a fear of success? There couldn't be. It doesn't add up. Everyone craves and longs for success, whatever that means to them. That is the very definition of success. Something you crave and long for. Therefore it can't be something you fear, otherwise you're just saying that language doesn't mean anything. So why do people embrace this fake fear and add it to their long list of real fears?

Maybe it's code for the real fear. The real fear might really be that I'd have to make a prolonged effort at mastering something in order to be successful. And I don't think I'm up to it. If people were honest they'd just say that.

And then a coach like you or me would help them see that OF COURSE YOU ARE UP TO IT!! YOU LEARNED TO WALK AND TALK DIDN'T YOU?

Walking and talking were harder to master than anything you wish you could master and be successful at right now. It's just that those skills were learned early on . . . back in the days when you weren't a self-conscious personality . . . back in the days of joy when there was no possibility of "losing face." Or, "being a loser." Or embarrassing your "self."

No, back then there was just adventure and exploration. There was just walking and talking. It happened wholeheartedly because there was no one—no painful, particular, separate, isolated, self-conscious individual— trying to do it. Trying to get it right.

We want that back, don't we? That spirit, and that inner, innate wisdom that had us learning so fast as a child.

Picasso said, "Once I drew like Raphael but it has taken me a lifetime to draw like a child."

It took him a lifetime to get it back. Maybe we can get it back faster than he did. Are you up for right now? Being as you were as a child, fearlessly exploring?

There was also no ownership of fear back then. Oh, yes, there was fear. And it came and went (like it does today). But it wasn't a permanent possession like people say it is today. It wasn't experienced as My Fear.

This was a revelation to me. Seeing this in my own life. And it's revealing something to me every time I reflect on it. It wasn't that I was purer or better or more enlightened as a child. It's just that I hadn't gotten into personal accumulation and possessiveness yet. I hadn't created an identity.

There's good news in this for me. It shows me where I went wrong. The path I took that had me see everything from inside the stifling clown suit I called my permanent personality. Didn't I just make that personality up? Didn't I just create that separate identity out of nothing? Isn't the clown suit just for the birthday party? Do I really have to wear it everywhere I go?

Almost everyone I've ever met has this sense of ownership around fear. They make something temporary a permanent part of who they are. And they don't stop there. Because I also notice that almost everyone I've ever known constantly uses the phrase "one of my biggest fears." I might ask them about why they look worried and they say, "One of my biggest fears is that . . ." and they talk about what might occur.

If I am constantly saying "One of my biggest fears . . ." it means that not only do I have a lot of fears, but that many are big fears and I'm about to reveal to you one (just one for now) of the biggest. I mean, we're now talking about one of the biggest of the big that I own. That's how we talk. That's what we say.

Soon I began to get the feeling that deep down life was better than how we talk about it and what we say it is.

A political victory, a rise of rents, the recovery of your sick, the return of your absent friend, or some other favorable event raises your spirits, and you think good days are preparing for you. Do not believe it. Nothing can bring you peace but yourself. Nothing can bring you peace but the triumph of principles.

~ Ralph Waldo Emerson
Self-Reliance

Just Looking for a Home

The philosopher Martin Heidegger said, "Language is the house of being. In its home human beings dwell."

So let's look at this old house. What do we say in language that gives us our current sense of home? Let's start with something I used to say (and think and believe) that kept me trapped in an old dwelling that was too small and always felt unsafe.

Not only did I used to say, "One of my biggest fears . . ." all the time but I noticed that I was also always saying, "Part of me wants to . . ."

Part of me wants to do this and part of me wants to do that.

I wasn't alone. I was hearing that phrase from everyone I knew!

So what's wrong with always saying, "Part of me wants to . . ."? As in, "Part of me wants to just quit this job and get a small place in the country and raise little lambs."

It's not wrong. But my experience now tells me that it's inaccurate. It produces an unnecessary limitation on our experience of life.

Is there *really* a fixed piece of you that wants to do

something? Tell the truth. Where is that part? Is it in your heart? In your head? And how big is it? How many other parts are there? Do they want other things?

"Yes!" you say. "Part of me wants to learn to enjoy the work I have and not fantasize about leaving."

Okay. You've got two parts now, in conflict with each other, but still always there. They must always be there because you believe they are a part of you. And your parts, when you add them up, make up the whole you. A big, dense permanent you.

And that's it for you. You're complete. Now you've got to work with what permanent parts you've got! Right?

Not right. Because you've made yourself into a construction. A limited number of parts and pieces permanently cemented together into you. So when Patsy Cline sings "I Fall to Pieces" it means something to you. It touches your heart . . . the part that's your heart. You identify. This assembled identity could someday fall to pieces.

I understand this line of thought. I was there too. But to me, this eventually got exposed as the most irrational and unjustifiably limiting self-concept I could have come up with. It was a self-concept I perpetuated with my language.

Fortunately I have found another way to look at this. This thing called life. This thing called me. The new look requires that I am willing to see a thought for what it is. Passing through. Not permanent. Not personal, even. And this perspective allows me a new place to look from that feels closer to the truth about what's really happening in the universe. It also feels freer. This new look might have me say, "Sometimes I get a thought about moving to the country. Then I get a picture of nature, and a garden and sheep, and it feels peaceful and simple and free."

Do I want to do anything with this thought? Maybe. I

could trap it like a butterfly and pin its wings down so I can study it further. Maybe I'll do that! And maybe I won't. Because here comes a new thought and it might be even better than that one.

There's freedom in that experience. A spaciousness and spiritual energy. There is a lightness in simply noticing a thought I'm seeing right now, instead of the heaviness I feel when I believe there's a solid permanent part of me (that wants something!). I don't really want to walk around feeling heavy and permanent. I'm happier when I see that I'm an open house. I entertain all thoughts that arrive. They aren't ponderous parts of me.

In fact this house doesn't even need walls. It's open to everything. Sometimes I like to imagine that thoughts are God whispering in my ear. Sweet nothings. They come and they go.

When God whispers, "What do you want to do today?" I don't say, "A part of me wants to do X! But I know I really should . . ." When God whispers, "What do you want to do?" I might just say, "I don't know. Inspire me."

All the world's a stage…

~ William Shakespeare
As You Like It

No Idea Who Spartacus Is

Sometimes I like to quote Werner Erhard to clients (and even friends looking for help). I especially like to pass on his wisdom about choosing to be "cause in the matter" of their lives.

My friend, whom I'll call Tanya, was confused about this idea after we talked about it because she wondered about all the things truly out of her control, like the death of a family member, and learning to accept and love "What Is." It was hard for her to reconcile that with being the cause in all matters of her life.

I asked if she'd ever seen the movie *Spartacus*.

"Yes, ages ago."

We talked about the movie and she remembered the scene where the Roman guards came to take away the galley slave Spartacus for crucifixion, and before he could identify himself many of the other slaves, one at a time, stepped up and said, "I am Spartacus!"

It was a moving moment in the film, but what I wanted Tanya to see was the power of their declaration, "I am Spartacus!" By declaring that, the Romans had no idea who the real Spartacus was.

Well, the slaves who yelled that phrase weren't *really* Spartacus. It wasn't true, what they said. But it was powerful. And it got the job done. Which was my point in asking her to recall that scene. It doesn't have to be *true* that you are the cause of your life for you to gain benefit from saying it. This is a game we're playing here.

Werner Erhard says, "That you are the *cause* of everything in your life is a place to stand from which to view and deal with life—a place that exists solely as a matter of your choice. The stand that one is *cause in the matter* is a declaration, not an assertion of fact."

The key words there are "not an assertion of fact." In other words it's not a fact that you cause everything, and he's clear about that. Tanya had already seen that it wasn't a fact that she was the cause of everything. She was even happy about it. She felt how healthy it was to be at peace with whatever happened and welcome reality in. Some say this awareness grants us "the serenity to accept the things I cannot change." It's healing.

BUT what Werner is saying (and I am saying) is that a declaration (I am CAUSE) can be extremely useful "as a place to stand from." A role you can play. A place you can come from. Out in the game of life, when you're playing that game in society and with other people.

When I first learned this idea of "being cause in the matter" of my life it was a turning point. I had always felt I was merely at the mercy of outside forces. In my mind, everything in the world marketplace was about luck and privilege. And when I heard stories of people working their way up from nothing I believed they had self-motivation in their DNA and I didn't. From an early age I also believed that grownups had all the money and all the power and I knew I would never grow up. I was a poster boy for a victim mindset and a permanent case of arrested development.

And it turns out that I was truly an extreme case. My belief system led to hugely dysfunctional interaction with the real world. Or lack of interaction, depending how you see it. Lack of action, for sure. My being the effect and not the cause resulted in a kind of spiritual atrophy. I was overcome with weakness. In my real world there were huge breakdowns. I ended up dealing with (and feeling like a victim of) bankruptcy, divorce, alcoholism . . . and we could go on.

Dr. Martin Seligman's studies refer to a life like mine as "learned helplessness."

Fortunately the mentoring I got from 12-Step sponsors, teachers and then coaches saved me. That and the books I started reading. They led me to the option I never knew I had. This option was that I could declare myself to be cause in the matter of my life. My business consultant and life coach at the time, Steve Hardison, actually had the word CAUSE on his car's license plate. So he was an effective advocate.

Soon I found that by coming from that place, from declaring that I was cause, I could make things happen. And the joy was that it was not my personality doing it. In a funny way, it was not even about me.

It was the stand itself.

The stand was enough. I didn't have to wonder if "I" had what it took. I didn't have to worry about my permanent identity and whether that person could ever make anything happen. The stand itself (coming from a created place inside of me that declared that I was cause) was more than enough to start me on the path of getting my whole life turned around.

It was a way to play the game.

No one I've met since those days has had a case of victim

mindset quite as severe as mine was. But almost all people have *some* version of it that keeps them from enjoying the game and playing it wholeheartedly. And it's no wonder that almost everyone has a touch of this. The movies, the media, most parents, most everyone in the culture teach us to get used to being at the mercy of circumstance. All power seems to be *out there* in the hands of events, companies, politicians and other people. We learn that. It's deeply drilled into us.

But when I decide that I want to create a business or make my relationships better this declaration of being cause helps clear my head and gets me connected to the real creative power of life (within me). Standing as cause helps me sort out my day. It shows me what to focus on. It gives me strength and the glory of simplicity.

Believe in a love that is being stored up for you like an inheritance, and have faith that in this love there is a strength and a blessing so large that you can travel as far as you wish without having to step outside it.

~ Rainer Maria Rilke

How Do You Master This?

I imagine people wondering how I could possibly believe that you could "master" the beauty of the present moment. They would tell me that the present moment is a beauty to be felt, not mastered.

Mastery suggests the action of doing things and practicing a craft or skill.

But I'm leaving the phrase like it is because I just like it. It doesn't make logical sense, but it feels good when I say it. It reminds me of when people say something like, "Hey, let's do Vegas!" Las Vegas is a place you visit, not an action you take. It's not a thing you do. If I were teaching a basic English class I'd make that point to the students.

But the phrase is still good to say! "Hey, we're three sheets to the wind and halfway across the Arizona desert . . . we might as well do Vegas!"

In that same spirit I like the thought that I'm going to wake up today and master some beauty! That stupid phrase makes happiness, fulfillment and thriving feel doable to me, and without that feeling I'd have given up long ago.

Yes, I see that there isn't anything I have to *do* to enjoy the beauty of the now. And I also see that the present moment, when fully relaxed into, is blissfully timeless and eternal.

But there's more to it than that. If there weren't, the present moment would start to resemble a vacant kind of emptiness. Like being on heroin.

So there's more: The present moment is both perfect as it is, *and is full of possibility.*

Both things!

Steve Hardison used to show me this paradox by banging a table with his hand and saying it seemed to be a solid thing—Whap! Whap! Whap!—but looked at another way, it was nothing but an empty dancing swirl of energy waves. Both solid and empty. Both. At the same time.

So knowing life is inherently perfect and then wanting to create a better life works for me. Why not create better products, services, relationships, songs and prosperity? New partnerships among nations! It can all go together.

Loving what is and making things better. They can go together. Like truth and beauty. Like beauty and truth.

No valid plans for the future can be made by those who have no capacity for living now.

~ **Alan Watts**

Is There Life After High School?

There have been books written on this subject, some with the exact title of this chapter, and the conclusion is . . . basically? No.

In other words we don't change much after that. Who we were in high school is likely to be who we are now.

Unless, of course, we are willing to see through all of this play acting we do. Not making it wrong, because it lets us play on the stage of society with all the other actors. But seeing it (and enjoying it) for what it is.

My suspicion is that high school is where we completed work on the creation of our personalities. No, even deeper than personalities . . . on what we thought were our very identities as separate selves in the world. The goal of each of these character-creations in high school was to avoid embarrassment. In high school there was no pain as great as embarrassment. We'd rather receive a full-on oncological radiation treatment than to blush with embarrassment.

Why? Because that was the time when our teenage hormones were surging. So the mission of being liked and admired, or at least accepted and appreciated, was the most important thing in the whole world. It was foremost in our minds throughout the livelong day.

Who will you be to avoid embarrassment? *Who will you be* in order to be liked? Some of us chose to shrink back and become shy and humble characters. That felt safe. Others needed to pump up the volume and be big and extroverted to cover their insecurity. Whatever seemed to work!

All of that activity was understandable. It was our abrupt entry into the social world and we would have to learn to survive.

But there was a problem with this process of character-creation in those formative years. The problem was that we inevitably believed our own act.

We eventually thought that who we were creating ourselves to be was actually not an invention, but rather a permanent set of pre-existing characteristics and qualities. So as the years went by those characteristics were given more and more significance and permanence.

And then it felt solidified. Not only did we think our characteristics were real and hardwired, we started to believe that they were even causative! They caused our behavior! We started using our characteristics to explain everything! I am not a detail person! I'm an introvert! I'm not good with languages! I'm not good at dating! I'm a cake person!

It's as if we all were assigned parts in the school play and then couldn't stop being that character long after the play was over. Forgetting completely that it was just a play. (A musical comedy if we look back honestly.)

Soon all our actions were based on the characteristics of the person we made up. We didn't see that our actions *could* spring from the opportunity that called to us in the present moment. We missed the beauty of the present moment entirely because our focus was on who we thought we were and what the characteristics of that person were causing to happen.

From that delusion it was hard to create loving, lasting relationships. Because, as Byron Katie says, "Personalities don't love—they want something."

But sometimes . . . and not very often . . . sometimes we got glimpses of the truth.

We'd see someone across a crowded room at the prom and our heart would stop. Our thoughts about ourselves would disappear and it felt like we were in heaven. What was happening? Were we falling in love?

Maybe what really stopped at that moment wasn't the heart. What if what stopped was just all those thoughts? All those thoughts that were headed for the future or else going into the past.

What if when the truth (beauty) is glimpsed those thoughts fall away? And love is just the beauty arising out of feeling the here and now.

When you've said all of the bad things and all of the good things you haven't been saying, you will find that what you've really been withholding is, "I love you." You don't have to go looking for love when it is where you come from.

~ **Werner Erhard**

Recommended . . .

Reading

Coming Home by Dr. Dicken Bettinger and Natasha Swerdloff
One Thought Changes Everything by Mara Gleason
Creating the Impossible by Michael Neill
Loving What Is by Byron Katie
A Thousand Names for Joy by Byron Katie
Prison Break by Jason Goldberg
The Little Book of Big Change by Amy Johnson
The Essential Colin Wilson by Colin Wilson
Straight-Line Leadership by Dusan Djukich
The Relationship Handbook by George and Linda Pransky
The Path of No Resistance by Garret Kramer
The Religion of Tomorrow by Ken Wilber

Events

Jason Goldberg's cross-country JoyRide:
http://www.ProjectJoyRide.com

Music

Fred Knipe's album: *9Ninety9*.

About the author

Steve Chandler has written dozens of books on subjects that swing dizzyingly from Jane Austen to baseball to business coaching to travel to obituaries to Moby Dick. He is the author of the bestsellers *Crazy Good* and *Time Warrior*.

He lives in Birmingham, Michigan, with his wife and editor, Kathy, and two hell hounds.

You may find him and learn of his latest adventures at www.stevechandler.com.

Books by Steve Chandler

Death Wish
Crazy Good
37 Ways to BOOST Your Coaching Practice
Wealth Warrior
Time Warrior
The Life Coaching Connection
Fearless
The Woman Who Attracted Money
Shift Your Mind Shift the World
17 Lies That Are Holding You Back
10 Commitments to Your Success
Reinventing Yourself
The Story of You
100 Ways to Motivate Yourself
How to Get Clients
50 Ways to Create Great Relationships
The Joy of Selling
Powerful Graceful Success
RelationShift (with Michael Bassoff)
The Small Business Millionaire (with Sam Beckford)
100 Ways to Create Wealth (with Sam Beckford)
9 Lies That Are Holding Your Business Back
(with Sam Beckford)
Business Coaching (with Sam Beckford)
100 Ways to Motivate Others (with Scott Richardson)
The Hands Off Manager (with Duane Black)
Two Guys On the Road (with Terrence Hill)
Two Guys Read the Box Scores (with Terrence Hill)
Two Guys Read Jane Austen (with Terrence Hill)
Two Guys Read Moby Dick (with Terrence Hill)
Two Guys Read the Obituaries (with Terrence Hill)
The Prosperous Coach (with Rich Litvin)

Audio by Steve Chandler

9 Lies That Are Holding Your Business Back
10 Habits of Successful Salespeople
17 Sales Lies
37 Ways to BOOST Your Coaching Practice (audiobook)
Are You A Doer Or A Feeler?
Challenges
Choosing
Crazy Good (audiobook)
Creating Clients: Referrals
Creating Clients: The 18 Disciplines
Creative Relationships
Death Wish (audiobook)
Expectation vs. Agreement
Fearless (audiobook)
Financially Fearless
How To Double Your Income As A Coach
How to Get Clients (audiobook)
How To Help A Pessimist
How To Solve Problems
Information vs. Transformation
Is It A Dream Or A Project?
Making A Difference
MindShift: The Steve Chandler Success Course
Ownership And Leadership
People People
Personality Reinvented
Purpose vs. Personality
Serving vs. Pleasing People
Testing vs. Trusting
The Creating Wealth audio series
The Fearless Mindset
The Focused Leader

The Function Of Optimism
The Joy Of Succeeding
The Owner / Victim Choice
The Prosperous Coach (audiobook)
The Ultimate Time Management System
Time Warrior (audiobook)
Wealth Warrior (audiobook)
Welcoming Every Circumstance
Who You Know vs. What You Do
Why Should I Reinvent Myself?
You'll Get What You Want By Asking For It

Publisher's Catalogue

Devon Bandison

Fatherhood Is Leadership: Your Playbook for Success, Self-Leadership, and a Richer Life

Sir Fairfax L. Cartwright

The Mystic Rose from the Garden of the King

Steve Chandler

37 Ways to BOOST Your Coaching Practice: PLUS: the 17 Lies That Hold Coaches Back and the Truth That Sets Them Free

50 Ways to Create Great Relationships

Business Coaching (Steve Chandler and Sam Beckford)

Crazy Good: A Book of CHOICES

Death Wish: The Path through Addiction to a Glorious Life

Fearless: Creating the Courage to Change the Things You Can

RIGHT NOW: Mastering the Beauty of the Present Moment

The Prosperous Coach: Increase Income and Impact for You and Your Clients (Steve Chandler and Rich Litvin)

Time Warrior: How to defeat procrastination, people-pleasing, self-doubt, over-commitment, broken promises and chaos

Wealth Warrior: The Personal Prosperity Revolution

Kazimierz Dabrowski

Positive Disintegration

Charles Dickens

A Christmas Carol: A Special Full-Color, Fully-Illustrated Edition

Anthony Drago

Go Prove Something! A Basketball Player's Guide to Legally Using PEDs

James F. Gesualdi

Excellence Beyond Compliance: Enhancing Animal Welfare Through the Constructive Use of the Animal Welfare Act

Janice Goldman

Let's Talk About Money: The Girlfriends' Guide to Protecting Her ASSets

Christy Harden

Guided by Your Own Stars: Connect with the Inner Voice and Discover Your Dreams

David Lindsay

A Blade for Sale: The Adventures of Monsieur de Mailly

Abraham H. Maslow

The Psychology of Science: A Reconnaissance

Being Abraham Maslow (DVD*)*

Maslow and Self-Actualization (DVD)

Albert Schweitzer

Reverence for Life: The Words of Albert Schweitzer

Margery Williams

The Velveteen Rabbit: or How Toys Become Real

Colin Wilson

New Pathways in Psychology: Maslow and the Post-Freudian Revolution

Join our Mailing List:

www.MauriceBassett.com

MAURICE BASSETT
books for athletes of the mind

Made in the USA
Columbia, SC
11 September 2017